Floorcloth Magic

Floorcloth Magic

How to Paint Canvas Rugs for Decorative Home Use

Lisa Curry Mair

Photographs by Giles Prett
(except as noted)

STOREY BOOKS

North Adams, Massachusetts

The mission of Storey Publishing is to serve our customers by publishing practical information that encourages personal independence in harmony with the environment.

Edited by Deborah Balmuth and Karen Levy
Cover and interior design by Alexis Siroc
Photo styling by Lisa Curry Mair and Karen Levy
All floorcloth designs (except where noted) by Lisa Curry Mair
Art direction and design modifications by Cynthia McFarland
Text production by Susan Bernier and Jennifer Jepson Smith
Indexed by Deborah Burns

Storey Books are available for special premium and promotional uses and for customized editions. For further information, please call Storey's Custom Publishing Department at (800) 793-9396.

Printed in Hong Kong by C&C Offset Printing Co., Ltd.
10 9 8 7 6 5 4 3 2 1

Library of Congress Cataloging-in-Publication Data

Mair, Lisa Curry.
    Floorcloth magic : how to paint canvas rugs for decorative home
use / by Lisa Curry Mair.
        p. cm.
    ISBN 1-58017-405-1 (alk. paper)
    1. Painting 2. Floor coverings I. Title
    TT385 .M34 2001
    746.6—dc21
                                                              2001040096

Contents

Dedication

*To the memory of
Mary Hoag Lawrence*

Acknowledgments

I thank my husband, Bart,
and daughter, Lauren,
for their endless encouragement
and for their
amazing ability to
always make me smile.

History of Floorcloths

FLOORCLOTHS ARE MADE OF heavyweight cotton canvas, a few latex paint colors, and a coat or two of polyurethane sealer. These simple, practical floor coverings are extremely useful in a wide range of rooms throughout the home. From grand entryways to contemporary kitchens, cheerful sunrooms to classic dining rooms, kids' rooms to bathrooms, floorcloths fit in beautifully everywhere. They are easy to make, instantly gratifying, and incredibly long lasting. Best of all, they are a perfect combination of a practical object — something to cover a floor — and a creative way to make a personal artistic mark.

FLOORCLOTHS HAVE BEEN USED in homes throughout the United States for hundreds of years. The first American settlers were intent on decorating their new dwellings to remind them of their homes across the sea.

Because resources were limited, they used their ingenuity to make floor coverings when carpets were unavailable. Worn sails from ships supplied them with canvas; hand-cut stencils and freehand painting provided pattern and color. The designs were sealed with varnish and became known as *oyl clothes,* or floorcloths.

Floorcloths were placed over existing carpets and used as "crumb catchers." They also served to reduce drafts on wide-board floors. Being cool underfoot, painted canvases often replaced wool and rag rugs during the summer months.

Drawings; paintings; and early records of household inventories, business directories, and advertisements show evidence of floorcloth use. William Burnet, the governor of Massachusetts in the early 1700s, had a floorcloth listed in his household inventory, as did Robert "King" Carter, a colonial dignitary from Virginia. In 1796, records indicate that George Washington purchased a floorcloth for his Mount Vernon retirement home.

Until the end of the eighteenth century, floorcloths for wealthy homes were generally ordered and shipped from England. By the beginning of the nineteenth century, however, professional house and ship painters were creating them in the United States.

These painters used a variety of designs. Marbled, geometric designs were popular for entryways, parlors, and dining rooms, while solid colors and freehand paintings of animals and flower motifs were common in less formal sitting rooms. More intricate designs included faux Brussels carpets and Turkish rugs, since the real ones were so expensive. In rural areas, itinerant artisans used hand-cut stencils and simple freehand designs to make floorcloths for homes throughout the countryside.

An 1809 inventory of the White House includes, for the south dining-room, "a canvas floor-cloth, painted green."

Floorcloths Today

It's little wonder that our ancestors found floorcloths so appealing, and they continue to make wonderful floor coverings in today's homes, as well. By coordinating colors and designs with existing elements in a room, floorcloths provide a way to tie the floor in with the rest of the space. Since they wipe clean and stand up to the toughest of foot traffic, kids can spill grape juice and spaghetti sauce and dogs can chase toys under the table without you worrying that they'll stain or scratch the surface.

Floorcloths make a graceful — or bold or humorous — statement. A design of bright checks in an entryway welcomes visitors. A whimsical pattern of fruit and flowers looks great in front of a kitchen sink or stove. Hallways, enclosed porches, and bathrooms are wonderful spaces for bright, cheerful floor art. In larger areas, simple geometric designs can help unite a room's color scheme while defining distinct sections, such as a dining area within a large kitchen or family room. Floorcloths also make great gifts, especially when painted to coordinate with the recipient's tastes in color and design.

Once you get started, it will be hard to stop. You will find uses for floorcloths in almost every room of your home. With a little observation and some imagination, you'll discover inspiration for colors, textures, and designs within your home as well as outside it.

The following chapters will show you everything you need to know to design, paint, and create your own durable, beautiful floorcloths. They also showcase the imaginative diversity this craft inspires in a variety of artists.

American Primitive painting Girl with a Dog, *circa 1800, shows a Carwitham floorcloth design. (From the collection of the Abby Aldrich Rockefeller Folk Art Museum, Williamsburg, VA.)*

JOHN CARWITHAM'S DESIGNS FROM THE 1700S

In 1739, the London engraver John Carwitham published 24 plates of designs for floorcloths and other floor decorations. His designs were geometric layouts of squares, diamonds, hexagons, and octagons in various arrangements. Some were flat two-dimensional patterns, while others were more complicated three-dimensional designs. Most of his designs included marbling and other textural techniques, which were commonly used to replicate expensive stone and parquet floors. Even now, these designs complement a room full of antiques or, if painted in a bolder color palette, look great with all kinds of contemporary furnishings.

Floorcloths Underfoot

TODAY, MORE AND MORE BUILDERS are installing wood, tile, and laminate floors throughout newly built homes. This is partially an aesthetic trend, but it is also an environmental one. Many homeowners are concerned about health issues surrounding synthetic carpets and the glues that affix them to subfloors. Allergies and respiratory problems are on the rise, leading us to search for cleaner, healthier alternatives for interior decorating materials.

While bare floors are beautiful, they long for areas of color and pattern to break up their expanse in large rooms. Traditional oriental, braided, and hooked rugs serve the purpose but are expensive, fragile, and difficult to clean. What is the solution? A painted canvas floorcloth. It will slide right in and make itself at home, standing up to years of heavy traffic and wiping clean with a damp mop. Add to that the opportunity to express your creative side, and you've got the perfect covering for any floor.

The Benefits of Floorcloths

Floorcloths have numerous benefits. They are easy to keep clean, tough as nails, and fun to paint. Furthermore, they add that definitive appeal that only a piece of handcrafted artwork can provide. Floorcloths look great on any type of floor — particularly wood — and can even be used to cover an unsightly subfloor.

When you consider the dust, pet hair, and microscopic organisms that can build up in the tiny fibers of wall-to-wall carpets, it's little wonder that allergies and respiratory problems are so prevalent today. Even the most diligent housekeeper armed with a heavy-duty vacuum cleaner has trouble winning the war against tiny carpet dwellers. Add to this the powerful fumes emitted by epoxies used to glue the carpet in place, and you've got a potential health hazard right under your feet.

On the other hand, floorcloths have a finished, washable surface but still retain some carpet-like qualities. They muffle sound, provide a little warmth to a cold floor, and add color and pattern to a room. You can sweep them, vacuum them, and even scrub them with disinfecting soap. If you use latex and other water-based paints and sealers, the finished pieces have little or no odor.

Floorcloths hold up to even the heaviest of foot traffic. Dogs tearing into the house from outdoors, spills from food and drink, roughhousing children, and heavy chairs pushed to and from the table do no harm to them, either. When they are placed on a hard surface, very little can scratch, dent, or even mar the durable polyurethane finish, which produces a heavy-duty plasticlike coating. A thick polyurethane finish applied over several coats of paint strengthens the surface while keeping it flexible. In addition, water-based polyurethane doesn't yellow like older varnishes tend to do, and it resists fading and cracking.

Best of all, floorcloths are easy to make. The same basic steps are used in every project. Prepare the canvas. Paint the floorcloth. Seal the finished piece. A craft doesn't get much simpler than that. In addition, the essential supplies are inexpensive and easy to find at paint, craft, and hardware stores. You probably already have a lot of the things you need to make a floorcloth right in your basement or garage.

A small basic floorcloth can be completed in a weekend and is ready to put into use a few days after that. It provides quick gratification for even the most impatient crafter. Chances are that, as you finish up your first floorcloth project, you will start thinking of other places in your home (or in somebody else's home) that are crying out for a floorcloth, as well.

Floorcloths accent almost any room's décor and are perfect under tables.

But Can I Walk on It?

The first question people invariably ask as they enter a floorcloth booth at a craft show for the first time is, "Are these to walk on?" We have been taught that art is to be hung on the wall or carefully placed on a table, but never soiled or used or touched. Old habits die hard, and allowing your creation to be stomped on does take a little getting used to. When you see first hand how durable and washable your floorcloth really is, you will join floorcloth artists in encouraging others to break with tradition and walk all over the artwork.

A Blank Canvas

Each floorcloth starts as, literally, a blank canvas. You can seal it and use it as is or, for a contemporary statement, paint one red dot in the corner and call it done. More likely, though, you will feel compelled to paint a design or a scene that is in some way an expression of yourself and your home.

If the idea of creating a design entirely from scratch seems overwhelming to you, then go ahead and copy something else. Before long, you will probably feel like changing a little here and a little there, hence the birth of your individual creativity! Use the many designs presented within this book as a starting point, and then move on from there. The possibilities for design and color are endless.

There's something about the large-scale nature of a floorcloth that seems to free up even the most artistically shy person. It's big and bold, and you'll drive yourself nuts if you worry about tiny details. Big brushes, lots of paint, and a large piece of canvas stretched out on the floor are an invitation to self-expression. Be brave. Jump in. And remember — if you don't like what you've done, you can always paint over it and start again.

Setting Up a Workspace

Making a floorcloth is not a difficult process, but it can be time consuming. Almost every step requires time to dry. In addition, it's important not to move the floorcloth during drying, and to leave it in a place where household members won't put things on top of it. The kitchen table may seem like a nice spot to work, but when the first person drops a magazine on your freshly painted design, you will probably regret selecting that workspace.

The ideal workspace is a large, sturdy table in a well-lit room with little to no traffic and a floor that doesn't mind a few splashes of paint. A card table set up in an out-of-the-way spot also works well for small projects. You can store your paints, brushes, and other project-related stuff in a box that slides under the table when not in use. For larger projects, you'll need a clean, flat surface in a dust-free room.

Another option is to paint the floorcloth on top of plastic sheeting in the room where it will reside. The added benefit of this method is being able to see how the lighting in the room affects the colors while the work is in progress. That way, you can make changes as you work.

My studio in Vermont has lots of light, a large table, and plenty of storage space for paints and brushes.

When working on the floor, be sure to use kneepads or a foam cushion as a kneeling pad to prevent your knee joints from pressing into a hard floor. However, if you have a history of back problems, avoid working on the floor, which can exacerbate the problem. A table at hip height — usually at least 32 inches (80 cm) above the floor — will reduce lower-back strain.

Preparation

After choosing your workspace, you will need to cover the painting area with plastic. Purchase rolls of 4-mil plastic sheeting at a hardware store. If you are using a table, cover the entire surface. Fold the plastic over the edges of the table and tape it securely to the underside. Stretch the plastic to smooth out any wrinkles, as these may cause ridges in the canvas later. When working on the floor, sweep or vacuum the entire area before putting the plastic sheeting down. Use masking tape to secure the entire edge of the canvas to the floor, again smoothing out any wrinkles as you go. Extend the plastic at least 12 inches (30 cm) on all sides beyond the size of the finished floorcloth.

PAINT QUALITY

In general, you get what you pay for. More expensive latex enamel lasts longer and performs better than low-grade paint. The latest innovations in latex paint make it comparable to oil-based paint in durability and flexibility, plus latex is much easier to clean up, faster drying, and more environmentally friendly.

Latex enamel is the best choice for floorcloths, as the plastics in the paint keep it flexible and less likely to crack when dry. You should also keep in mind that cheaper paint brands have more talc in their lighter colors (whites and pastels). This chalkiness leads to cracking. If you want to buy cheap paint, buy only dark-colored cheap paint.

Another way to save money is to ask the paint store whether they have any mistints, or paints that were returned by the customer because the color wasn't what they had expected. These cans are usually offered at a fraction of the original cost, and you can then tint the paint with tube acrylics to achieve the color you want.

Lighting and Ventilation

Set up lights that you can move as you work, so that you can see all areas of the floorcloth equally well. Proper lighting will also prevent eye strain as you work.

Daylight is the best sort of light when you are trying to analyze color combinations, but keep in mind that the room where the floorcloth will be used may not have good natural light. In that case, it's important to check color swatches in the light that is as close as possible to the lighting in the room. That way, you will avoid being surprised by how the room's lighting can change the colors of the finished piece.

If you will be using oil-based (alkyd) paints and sealers, good ventilation is an absolute necessity. Even water-based (latex) paints, and especially water-based polyurethanes, emit fumes that can cause headaches and blurred vision.

Don't take any chances. Use a strong fan, crack a window open, and wear a respirator, particularly when you are exposed to paint thinner or polyurethane for more than 10 minutes at a time.

Store the paint colors that you mix in small plastic containers with snap-on lids to reuse for other projects.

About Canvas

Canvas is woven from cotton thread of various thicknesses to create light-, medium-, and heavyweight cloth. You can buy canvas from art supply stores, fabric retailers, or awning and boat-cover manufacturers.

When you buy canvas, be sure to ask for 100% cotton, which is sometimes called *numbered duck*. The numbering system identifies the weight of the canvas. The greater the number, the lighter the weight.

For small floorcloths that are less than 3 feet by 4 feet (90 cm by 120 cm), #10 and #8 cotton duck are best. They are flexible, and the hem can be sewn with a standard sewing machine. If those weights are not available, you can use #12, but it will warp fairly easily and will wear out sooner than heavier canvases will.

For larger pieces, #8, #6, and #4 provide the best results. The heaviest canvas, #4, rarely warps and lies very flat. It's less prone to being kicked up at the corners, and it rarely needs to be adhered to the floor, especially if large furniture is placed on top. Most sewing machines that can sew through a few layers of denim can handle #4 with a heavy-duty needle, but you may want to try a small swatch on your machine before buying a big roll.

Purchasing Canvas

Raw canvas is a surprisingly delicate cloth. It will shrink, crease, buckle, and warp if you give it the chance. Creases can be particularly difficult to remove. Do not let the store fold your canvas. Have it rolled onto a tube to bring home. If you order by mail, ask the store to roll the canvas, otherwise they will usually fold it and push it into a box to ship.

To allow for shrinkage and hemming, buy at least 6 inches (15 cm) in all directions beyond the size of your finished floorcloth. For larger floorcloths, buy at least 12 inches (30 cm) more in all directions.

Primed "floorcloth" canvas is available at art supply stores. It is made of lightweight canvas that has been preshrunk and primed. Using primed canvas for your first project decreases the time spent preparing the canvas, but the end result is not as durable and the floorcloth may buckle. In addition, the weave on this lighter-weight canvas is not as prominent as it is on heavier cloth, so the painting techniques that are described in chapter 6 will have a more subtle effect. However, try experimenting with primed canvas scraps to practice various painting techniques and to see how the paint sits on the weave.

Canvas comes in different weaves and thicknesses, which affect the durability of your floorcloth.

THE QUEST FOR CANVAS

Heavyweight canvas can be difficult to find. Check the *Yellow Pages* for local manufacturers of handbags and awnings. Sailmakers sometimes use cotton canvas, but specify that you need cotton or they may supply you with a synthetic fabric that isn't as heavy and doesn't have the desired thickness.

CREASES

Even though a finished floorcloth is tough and durable, the raw canvas is very susceptible to creases and wrinkles. Do not attempt to clean the canvas in a washing machine. The spin cycle creates wrinkles that even the most persistent pressing cannot remove. There is no need to clean raw canvas. It will be covered with several layers of paint before it is sealed and put to use. Instead, remove loose dirt with a vacuum cleaner or lint remover.

Most canvas can be purchased in widths up to 10 feet (3 m). If you want to make an even larger floorcloth, you will need to piece two widths together. However, a sewn seam will be quite evident and create a ridge where the excess canvas is folded over. This can be avoided by butting the edges of the raw canvas together and carefully taping them with heavy-duty masking tape. Next, burnish the entire strip of tape with the back of a spoon to press the tape down into the weave. Then turn the canvas over and tape the front side, too. Don't worry — many layers of paint and sealer will hide the tape on the finished floorcloth.

Installing a Floorcloth

Newly painted floorcloths are easy to install, but allow the polyurethane to cure for at least a week before exposing the cloths to foot traffic. Floorcloths wear best on smooth, hard surfaces, such as hardwood, laminate, and vinyl flooring. They can also be used on cement, brick, and tile, but use a thin rubber, non-skid pad to keep the canvas from sinking into the grout and forming cracks in the surface.

Clean the floor well and make sure it is dry before placing a floorcloth on it. If the floorcloth is being used in front of a sink, in a hallway, or in a relatively open area, ensure that it is centered and square with the wall. Step back from it to make sure the location is pleasing.

Larger floorcloths used under tables and chairs do not need to be secured to the floor, especially if you used heavyweight canvas (at least #8) and if no warping occurred while you worked. However, if a corner of the floorcloth protrudes into a walkway, you'll need to secure that corner to prevent tripping. Floorcloths are extremely tough, but if they are folded, bent, or tripped over frequently, cracks will form and cause premature wear.

If the corner of a floorcloth may cause tripping or if a floorcloth will not have furniture placed on it, you will need to secure it to the floor, as the smooth surface of the back of the canvas can cause slipping. Not only can this damage your work of art, but it can also cause bodily harm. Mounting adhesive works well and doesn't damage the floor's finish.

Roll a small, pea-sized piece of the putty between your fingers and press it onto the back hem within ½ inch (1 cm) of the edge of the floorcloth. Continue pressing dots of adhesive every 3 inches (7.5 cm), making sure that the corners stick down firmly.

Walk on the edge of the floor-cloth to press the adhesive into the two surfaces. When you need to lift the floorcloth (to clean the floor beneath it or to move it to a new location), carefully pull the adhesive away from the floor. It will remain stuck to the floorcloth, since it sinks into the weave of the canvas, but it will lift right off the floor. For best results, remove as much of the used adhesive as you can and apply fresh adhesive when you reposition the floorcloth.

Caring for a Floorcloth

For day-to-day maintenance, sweep or vacuum dirt from the surface to prevent it from scratching the polyurethane finish. Damp mop when needed, using a mild deter-gent, like oil soap, then towel it dry to bring up a nice shine.

Occasionally, a coat of floor wax can be applied to restore the original luster. If the floorcloth is in a very high-traffic area, it may be necessary to apply a revitalizing coat of polyurethane annually. If you do so, clean the floorcloth well and remove any wax before apply-ing the polyurethane. Allow the polyurethane to dry for at least a week before putting the floorcloth back on the floor.

Mounting adhesive secures a floorcloth to the floor and prevents tripping.

It is possible to restore a worn floorcloth. If the paint has been worn through to the canvas, repaint the design. Match the colors as closely as possible, or repaint the entire surface to create a consistent color. If a small area has been dam-aged, it can be cleaned, bleached (if staining has occurred), repainted, and sealed.

To repair small holes, sand the paint immediately surrounding the opening. Cut a piece of masking tape ¼ inch (.5 cm) larger than the dam-aged area and press it into the hole with the back of a spoon. Repaint the area to match the design, then seal the entire floorcloth with several coats of polyurethane.

VINYL FLOORING FLOORCLOTHS

Have some fun playing with paint by creating a floorcloth on the reverse side of vinyl flooring. It is smooth and doesn't require any hemming or special preparation. You won't be able to produce the subtle effects that washes bring out in the distinct weave of heavy-weight canvas, but you can splash on some color and cut the vinyl into all kinds of shapes instead.

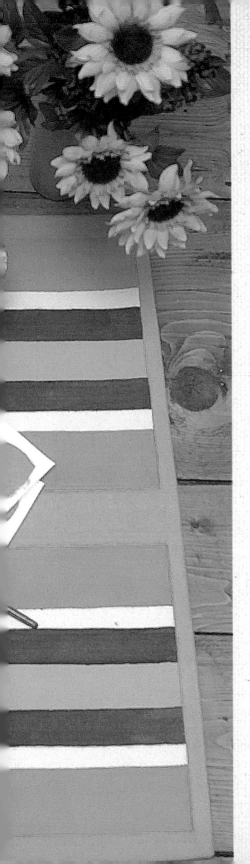

Ten Easy Steps

STARTING WITH A STRIKINGLY SIMPLE PATTERN on a relatively small piece of fabric, you'll learn the basics of canvas preparation, painting techniques, and finishing methods. The steps involved are simple and fun. Cut, press, and hem, then swipe on base coats and colorful strokes before adding a protective finish and *voilà*, your first "floor art masterpiece" is ready for action. Once you've completed the Basic Stripes floorcloth of 2 feet by 3 feet (60 cm by 90 cm), it will be perfect for all kinds of places in your home — in front of the kitchen sink, just inside the front door, or in a guest bath, to name a few. Then, armed with the knowledge of a few basic techniques, you will be ready to venture on to bigger and more complex floorcloth projects.

Getting Started

Before you begin, set up a workspace where you can leave the floorcloth to dry for several hours without being disturbed. This space should be dust free and well lit. A card table works well. Cover the surface with plastic and tape the edges of the plastic down to prevent slipping. See pages 8–10 for more information on setting up a workspace.

COLOR CHOICES

Use these colors or select your own combination using the color code below. Names of paint colors vary from brand to brand, so I won't use specific color names. Simply take this book to the paint store and match the swatches.

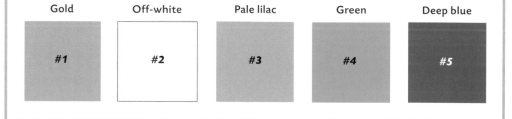

Gold	Off-white	Pale lilac	Green	Deep blue
#1	#2	#3	#4	#5

Step 1: Shrink the Canvas

Canvas is made of 100% cotton, so it will shrink significantly when painted. If the canvas is painted without prior shrinking, the floorcloth will warp, crease, and buckle, and the finished piece may end up several inches smaller than you intended.

MATERIALS
- Piece of lightweight canvas
- Large sponge
- Bucket of hot water
- Cardboard tube

Lay the canvas on the plastic and smooth it out as much as possible. With a large sponge, soak the canvas by scrubbing lots of hot water onto the entire surface. When the surface has been uniformly soaked, roll the wet canvas onto a tube and unroll it with the other side facing up. Soak the other side in the same manner. Leave the canvas flat and allow it to dry completely. Drying may take a day or two, depending on humidity.

Step 2: Cut the Canvas

Ever heard of the carpenter's maxim "measure twice, cut once"? It works. The time spent making a second careful measurement is never as frustrating as the time and expense wasted on an improperly cut piece of canvas.

MATERIALS
- Preshrunk canvas
- Long straightedge
- Pencil
- Carpenter's square
- Fabric scissors

Lay the preshrunk canvas on the table so that the longer side is closest to you. Using a long straightedge (use a board when a yardstick isn't long enough) and a pencil, draw a straight line about 1 inch (2.5 cm) in from and parallel to the long edge.

With a carpenter's square, make a second line perpendicular to the first, about 1 inch (2.5 cm) in from the rough edge of the canvas. Draw the second line the length of the short side of the finished floorcloth plus 2 inches (5 cm) for a total width of 26 inches (65 cm). Measure the first line and mark off 2 inches (5 cm) more than the desired long side, or 38 inches (95 cm). Use a carpenter's square to draw a third line up the other short side. Mark off 26 inches (65 cm). Now connect the two short sides and double-check the length of this fourth line. It should be 38 inches (95 cm). You will have marked a rectangle measuring 26 inches (65 cm) by 38 inches (95 cm). Make sure all the measurements are correct, and then cut the canvas with sharp fabric scissors, using long, firm strokes.

Step 3: Turn the Hem*

A nice clean hem is essential for a floorcloth to stand up to daily wear and tear. A well-made floorcloth lies flat on the floor with no warps or wrinkles. The edge of the floorcloth can be made three ways: with a sewn hem, with a glued hem, or with no hem at all. Steps 3 through 6 describe a machine-sewn hem that is prepared before the painting is started. A sewn hem gives extra thickness where the rug receives the most abuse. Glued hems and non-hemmed techniques, which are used after the floorcloth is painted and sealed with polyurethane, are discussed on page 28.

*Note: Sewing the hem is my preferred method for clean edges and a more durable floorcloth. If you do not want to sew the hem or are making a curved-edge floor-cloth, see Alternative Hemming Techniques on page 28. If you use one of those methods, skip Steps 3 through 6, continue the project at Step 7, and then hem the edges after you have painted the design and sealed the floorcloth (after Step 10).

Step 3: Turn the hem

MATERIALS
- Preshrunk, precut canvas
- Pencil
- Ruler
- Yardstick
- Iron
- Ironing board
- Sponge dipped in water

With a pencil, ruler, and yardstick, draw four lines 1 inch (2.5 cm) in from and parallel to the four cut edges of the floorcloth. These will be your folding lines. Preheat an iron to the hottest steam setting. Place one edge of the floorcloth on the ironing board with the pencil lines facing down. Run a damp sponge along both sides of the floorcloth edge, soaking the front and the back of the folding line. Turn the edge and press it with the iron so that the drawn line is at the fold. Repeat this on the other three edges, always turning the hem to the same side. Work slowly to ensure a good fold and be careful not to crease other areas of the floor-cloth as you work.

Step 4: Sew the Corners

Mitered corners are sewn corners that turn all the rough edges of the canvas inward. This makes a beautiful, clean edge that will not fray with use. It is well worth taking the extra time to sew these corners.

MATERIALS
- Pencil
- Preshrunk canvas with 1-in. (2.5 cm) hem pressed on all sides
- Ruler
- Straight pins
- Sewing machine
- Scissors
- Iron
- Spoon

Using a pencil on the canvas, place marks 1 and 2 where the two hems intersect (a).

Open the folds and place marks 3 and 4 on the reverse sides of the two marks you just made (b).

Bring marks 1 and 2 together until they touch. Marks 3 and 4 will be on the outside. With a ruler, draw a line perpendicular to the folded edge to mark 3 (c).

Place marks 1 and 2 where hems intersect

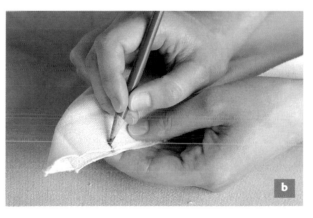

Open folds; place marks 3 and 4 on reverse side

Draw a line to the folded edge

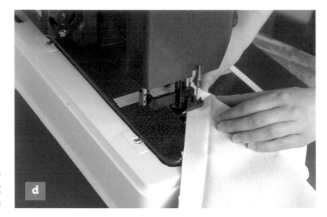

Stitch along the drawn line

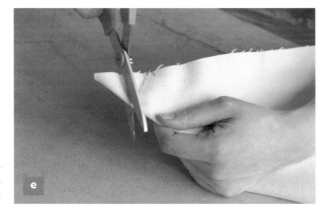

Cut away excess canvas

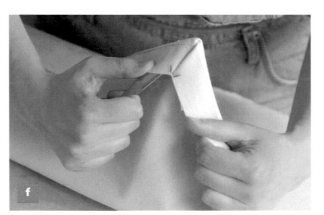

Turn corner right-side out

Step 4: Sew the Corners (*continued*)

Pin the corner securely in place. Repeat this entire procedure on the other three corners.

On a sewing machine, carefully stitch along the drawn line (d). Be sure to remove the straight pin just before sewing.

Cut away the excess canvas, being careful not to cut too close to the very tip of the corner (e). Use a hot iron to press the seam open so that it lies flat. Repeat these steps on the other three corners.

Turn the corner right side out. Use the handle of a spoon (or some other pointed object) to push out the fabric all the way and make a clean, square corner (f). Press the corner well with the iron on the highest setting. Repeat this process on the other three corners.

Step 5: Sew the Edges

A floorcloth made with sewn, mitered corners and a stitched hem will stand up to years of wear. Multiple coats of paint and polyurethane lock the threads in place, making it virtually impossible to pull the hem apart.

MATERIALS
- Sewing machine
- Canvas with sewn corners
- Ruler
- Scissors
- Iron

Using a straight, long stitch on a sewing machine, sew all the way around the perimeter of the floorcloth ⅝ inch (1 cm) in from the folded edge (a). Most sewing machines have a ⅝-inch guide marked on the throat plate to help you make a straight line of stitches, or you can draw a pencil line to indicate where to sew. Later, when the thread is painted, it will barely be noticeable. Trim away any stray threads with scissors.

Press the entire floorcloth to ensure crisp, flat edges and square corners (b).

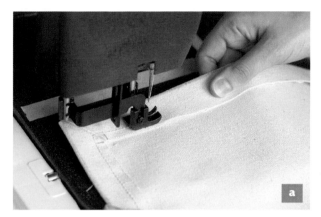

Sew around the perimeter of the floorcloth

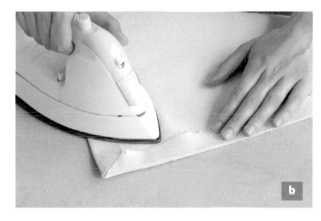

Press the entire floorcloth

PAINTING TIPS

- Always work in a well-ventilated area. Even latex paints contain fumes that can be harmful.

- Keep your brushes in good shape.

- If you have to stop painting to answer the phone or attend to another task, place the brush in a plastic container of water. When you return, wash the brush out with warm, soapy water, then squeeze out the excess water with a paper towel.

- Never leave your brushes in water overnight. The glue that holds the bristles in the metal ferrule will loosen, and the bristles will fall out.

- Do not leave brushes standing on their bristles, or they will bend. It is next to impossible to straighten a curled paintbrush.

- Don't load the brush with paint more than halfway up the bristles. If paint gets inside the ferrule, it is very difficult to clean the brush thoroughly.

- The plastic properties in latex paints are especially tough on brushes. Remove every trace of paint with warm soapy water before it has a chance to dry on the bristles.

- When you need just a small amount of paint, pour it into a clean, empty yogurt container. These are comfortable to hold in your non-painting hand and can be stored easily. The snap-on lids will keep paint from drying out for weeks.

- Store larger brushes by hanging them from a hook or nail with the bristles pointing down. Store smaller artist's brushes in a special brush caddie or a glass jar with the bristles pointing up.

Step 6: Paint the Hem

A painted hem prevents fraying and gives your floorcloth a continuous painted edge from front to back. The paint also stiffens the canvas and locks in the stitches on the hem.

MATERIALS
- Hemmed floorcloth
- Index card
- 1-in. (2.5 cm) latex paintbrush
- 1 cup (240 ml) latex enamel paint, color #1

Lay the floorcloth on the table with the back (and hem) facing up. Slide an index card under the hem at one of the corners. Using the 1-inch (2.5 cm) paintbrush, paint the hem color #1, sliding the index card along underneath the hem to prevent painting the back of the floorcloth.

When you've painted all the way around the hem, discard the index card and wash out the paintbrush. Let the hem dry for at least 3 hours before turning the floorcloth over.

Step 6: Paint the hem

Step 7: Apply the Base Coats

Applying two base coats to the right side of your floorcloth ensures an even application of the paint you will use for the design. The base coats stiffen the canvas and stabilize the surface for your painting. Use one of the colors of the design as a base coat to save yourself a step. Think about the best sequence of paint colors, then use the first (usually the background color) as the base coat color. For this project color #2 works well as a base coat.

MATERIALS

- Blank floorcloth with painted hem
- Lint remover roll
- 2-in. (5 cm) latex paintbrush
- 1 qt. (1 liter) flat finish latex enamel paint, color #2 (base coat)

When the hem is completely dry, turn the floorcloth over. With the lint remover, lift off all pieces of lint, dust, and stray threads of canvas from the front of the floorcloth.

Use the 2-inch (5 cm) latex brush to paint the entire surface of the floorcloth color #2. Start at the upper left corner and paint all the way down the short side, making about a 6-inch (15 cm) vertical strip, then move over to the next 6-inch (15 cm) segment. Continue painting in vertical bands until the entire surface is covered. Allow the floorcloth to dry overnight. Apply a second coat, keeping the brush strokes smooth and even, and again, allow the cloth to dry overnight.

Step 7: Apply base coats

Step 8: Transfer the design

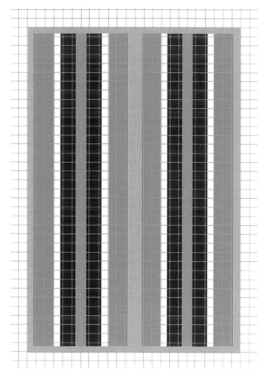

Basic Stripes Template
1 square = 1" (2.5 cm)

Step 8: Transfer the Design

With careful measuring, transferring a pattern from graph paper to canvas is easier than it looks. For clean, straight lines, keep your pencil sharp and hold the straight edge or yardstick firmly against the floorcloth.

MATERIALS

- Floorcloth with base coats applied
- Basic Stripes template
- Watercolor pencil
- Straight edge or yardstick
- Squeeze clamps
- Drawing triangle or a carpenter's square (optional)

Along the short sides of the floorcloth, make small but clear ticks for the stripes using the template at left (see page 130 for a larger pattern you can photocopy). Use a watercolor pencil so you can erase the lines with water, if necessary. Hold a yardstick firmly joining the tick marks and strike the lines to create the stripe pattern. If you need to, use squeeze clamps to firmly hold the yardstick on the floorcloth.

When laying out the pattern, double-check the squareness of the corners using a drawing triangle, a carpenter's square, or a yardstick and the 3-4-5 rule. Measure 3 inches (7.5 cm) from the corner to one edge and make a mark. From the same corner, measure 4 inches (10 cm) along the opposite edge and make a second mark. Now measure the distance between the two marks. It should be 5 inches (12.5 cm). If it isn't, go back and check that your right angles are 90 degrees.

This 3-4-5 rule works very well for larger floorcloths, where a slight degree off can throw a geometric design into chaos. Expand the measurements to 3 feet, 4 feet, and 5 feet (9 m, 12 m, and 15 m) to check for squareness in large floorcloths. Another trick for checking right angles is to measure across both diagonals. They should be equal.

Step 9: Paint the Design

In preparation for painting the stripes, make your work area as comfortable as possible. If your table is lower than hip level, you may want to sit on a stool or raise the table, so that you can stand to paint without putting strain on your back.

MATERIALS
- Floorcloth with transferred pattern
- Eraser
- Watercolor pencils
- Scrap canvas with base coats
- ½-in. (1 cm) flat bristle paintbrush
- Hair dryer
- Latex enamel paint, 1 cup (240 ml) *each* of colors #1, #3, #4, and #5
- Yardstick (optional)
- Permanent markers in the same colors as the paint (optional)

Erase any stray pencil marks on the floorcloth, so that you have a clear line to follow. The base-coat areas are

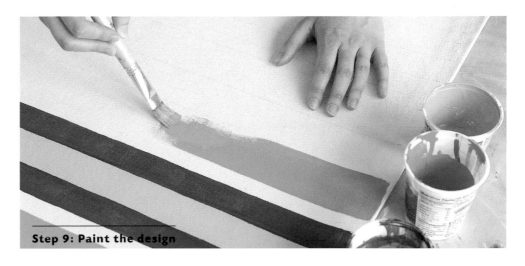

Step 9: Paint the design

already painted, so now you'll just be adding the stripes to create the pattern. To avoid making a mistake, code the lines with watercolor pencils to remind you which colors go on which stripes.

Practice making straight lines on some extra canvas that has two base coats of paint before attempting to paint a straight line on your floorcloth. If you have a steady hand and feel confident using a ½-inch (1 cm) flat bristle paintbrush, you can paint the stripes freehand.

Load the brush with paint about halfway up the bristles. Wipe one side of the brush on the edge of the paint can. Too much paint on the brush will be hard to control; too little will cause the paint to skip. Using the pencil marks as a guide, paint the edge of the line first, and then fill in with long, straight strokes. Apply all of the stripes of one color first, let them dry, and then apply the stripes of another color. Use a hair dryer to speed up the drying time. Apply one coat of colors #1, #3, #4, and #5.

Let the first coat of paint dry, then go over the solid colored areas with a second coat of all the colors to ensure a streak-free floorcloth. If you accidentally spill any drops of paint on a dry area, quickly wipe them up with a damp paper towel. You can also go over any mistakes with the appropriate color after the paint is thoroughly dry.

Apply a ½-inch (1 cm) border in color #1 around the entire edge of the floorcloth. Make sure you paint over the folded edge to make a continuous color from the front to the back of the floorcloth. Allow the first coat to dry before applying a second coat of paint, so that the border completely covers the stripe colors beneath.

If you don't feel comfortable painting freehand, you have a few options. You can simply not worry about painting straight lines at all and use big, bold, loose strokes to let the pattern be created by color. If you like the look of straight lines, you can hold a yardstick between the tick marks and use permanent markers in the same colors as the paint to draw the lines of the pattern. Then you can just fill in the lines with paint. Or you can use masking tape to create crisp lines.

How to Use Masking Tape

Some people find it easier to use masking tape to make clear lines, even if they have a steady hand. Others prefer to jump in and start painting without too much preparation work.

MATERIALS
- ½-in. (1 cm) masking tape
- Small craft knife
- Metal ruler
- Spoon

Apply the tape along the drawn lines, leaving the areas to be painted exposed. Press the tape securely down with the back of a spoon to keep paint from seeping underneath. Allow the paint to dry completely before removing the masking tape.

Applying masking tape guidelines

Step 10: Seal the Floorcloth

Allow the floorcloth to dry for at least 24 hours before you apply the polyurethane finish. Latex paint can take up to a week to dry completely, even though it is dry to the touch after an hour or so. The longer you allow the latex to dry, the less cracking you will see later.

MATERIALS
- Eraser
- Painted floorcloth
- Lint remover roll
- 1 qt. (1 liter) water-based polyurethane, satin finish
- 4-in. (10 cm) latex paintbrush

Erase any pencil marks that still remain on the floorcloth. Roll the lint remover over the entire surface to remove dust and eraser shavings. Stir the polyurethane thoroughly but gently, being careful not to add air bubbles. Using the 4-inch (10 cm) latex brush, start from the top left corner and work down, then across, the entire floorcloth.

Don't overwork the polyurethane. Use steady, even, smooth strokes to apply a nice, clear finish. Be sure to go right out to the edges, so that you totally seal all of the exposed paint surfaces. Apply at least three coats of polyurethane, allowing at least 12 hours of drying time between coats. Let the floorcloth cure for a week before putting it down on the floor. This will ensure that the latex has completely dried and that the polyurethane is sufficiently hardened.

Step 10: Seal the floorcloth

APPLYING POLYURETHANE

These tricks will help you apply an even, smooth finish to your floorcloth.

- Stir the polyurethane well, but gently. Be careful not to add air bubbles. Never let a paint salesperson shake your can of polyurethane. The bubbles will take days to subside.

- Apply the polyurethane with long strokes from a well-loaded brush. If the polyurethane starts to skip over the canvas (because there isn't enough loaded onto the brush), air bubbles will form. The trick is to apply the polyurethane in an even layer without overworking the surface.

- When you are using a quart-size can of polyurethane you may need to pour it into a plastic container with a wider mouth to accommodate the 4-inch (10 cm) paintbrush. A wide brush distributes the polyurethane more evenly.

- Don't be alarmed by the cloudy appearance. Polyurethane goes on cloudy and dries clear when it has been applied properly.

ALTERNATIVE HEMMING TECHNIQUES

If you choose not to sew the hem, you can glue it or have no hem at all. If you opt to use one of these techniques, skip Steps 3 through 6, continue the project from Step 7 through Step 10, and then finish the hem with one of these techniques.

A Glued Hem

Many professional floorcloth makers finish their cloths by gluing the hemmed edge instead of sewing it. This method is less time consuming than a sewn hem, but you will need to make or purchase a stretcher frame before you begin. Take care to make very clean, well glued, mitered corners, as there is a tendency for a tuft of canvas to work its way out of the corners. This will detract from the look of the finished piece and cause premature wear.

MATERIALS
- Canvas
- Thumbtacks or heavy-duty staple gun with ½-in. (12 mm) staples
- Wooden stretcher frame, 27 in. x 39 in. (67.5 cm x 97.5 cm)
- Pencil
- Scissors
- Rubber cement
- Spoon or tongue depressor

Cut the canvas 3 inches (7.5 cm) longer and 3 inches (7.5 cm) wider than the finished floorcloth will be. In this example, it should measure 27 inches by 39 inches (67.5 cm by 97.5 cm). Tack or staple the canvas at 1-inch (2.5 cm) intervals to a wooden stretcher frame. (Stretcher frames are available at art supply stores.) Start the project with Step 7 and continue through Step 10.

When the final coat of polyurethane is dry, remove the tacks or staples to release the floorcloth from the frame. On both sides of the floorcloth, draw a pencil line around the perimeter to form a 2-foot by 3-foot (60 cm by 90 cm) rectangle. This will be your fold line. Draw another line (either on the back or the front) 1 inch (2.5 cm) out from the fold line. This will be your cutting line. Use a sharp pencil so you can see the lines clearly.

Use scissors to cut away the edge that had the tacks in it, leaving the finished painting plus 1 inch (2.5 cm) around the entire fold line. Draw a diagonal line across each corner and through the point where the two fold lines intersect. Cut off the excess canvas. This creates the miter and prevents a lumpy corner.

Turn the floorcloth over. On the back, draw a gluing line 1 inch (2.5 cm) in from the fold line. Paint a layer of rubber cement from the gluing line out to the edge of the canvas on all four sides (a). Allow the cement to set until it is tacky. Apply a second coat and again allow it to dry until it is tacky.

a

Start turning the hem in the middle of one side of the floorcloth (b). Fold it along the fold line and burnish the hem with the back of a spoon or a tongue depressor.

Continue folding and pressing to the corner, then return to the middle and fold the hem to the opposite corner to complete that side (c). Be sure to press the corners down firmly. Repeat the gluing, folding, and burnishing with the other three edges and the corners to complete the floorcloth.

No Hem

To create an unusual, curvy-shaped floorcloth, you can skip the hemming process entirely. Be warned, however, that floorcloths made without a hem are more fragile and will warp along the edges if they are not prepared properly.

MATERIALS

- Heavyweight canvas
- Thumbtacks or heavy-duty staple gun with ½-in. (12 mm) staples
- Wooden stretcher frame, 30 in. x 42 in. (75 cm x 105 cm)
- Base paint
- 2-inch (5 cm) paintbrush
- Pencil
- Scissors
- Polyurethane

Use the heaviest canvas you can find and shrink it well. Allow it to dry thoroughly before you apply any paint. Tack or staple the canvas to the frame, which should be at least 6 inches (15 cm) larger than the finished floorcloth. If you will be cutting a curved or other non-straight edge, use a square or rectangular frame that covers the entire design. Apply several coats of base paint on both sides of the canvas, covering an area at least 4 inches (10 cm) larger than the design on all edges. On the face of the floorcloth, draw a light pencil line where you intend to cut the finished piece.

Paint the entire design and seal the floorcloth (Steps 7 through 10), as with other floorcloths. Later, when you remove the canvas from the frame, cut along the edge of the design. Apply an extra coat of polyurethane, being careful to seal the edge of the canvas.

No Hem: Cut along edge of design

Patterns and Borders

SINCE MOST FLOORCLOTHS are executed on a fairly large scale, the design is crucial. Filling a large, blank canvas with an arrangement of pattern and color that you can live with underfoot for years to come is one of the most interesting aspects of the design process. Make your big design decisions (and mistakes) on paper. In general, the time spent working out a design is worth every minute, as it will make you confident and relaxed about painting your floorcloth.

With a big, blank canvas staring back at you, design possibilities can seem overwhelming. In this chapter, you will learn how to break a big project down into small, manageable parts. Once you've worked out the perfect design, you'll transfer the finished layout to your blank floorcloth, bringing you one step closer to completing your own piece of floor art unique to your home and lifestyle.

Making Basic Decisions

Before you jump right in and start painting a floorcloth, you'll need to make several basic decisions, such as the location, size, design, and scale of your floorcloth.

Once you have decided to make a floorcloth for your home, the first question to ask yourself is, "Where will it go?" Perhaps a better question is, "Which part of my home needs a floorcloth the most?" Look for bare areas that need a splash of color or are showing signs of wear due to heavy traffic. Would a small spill-catching floorcloth in front of the kitchen sink be useful? Or would you rather go for an entry-

way pattern, to welcome visitors to your home?

If this is your first attempt, keep it as simple as possible. Remember that floorcloths do not wear well when placed on top of deep carpets and are best suited for wood floors.

Select the Size

Having chosen the space for your floorcloth, it's time to select the size that will best fit that location. Use masking tape to mark off the area you think will work best. Walk around, spend a day with your taped-off measurements, and determine whether this size is going to work for you. Adjust the tape and walk around some more until you find the optimum size and shape for that given space.

You may decide that the best floorcloth for your chosen area is not a rectangle. Perhaps a square, octagon, or other shape will work better. If you plan to hem your floorcloth, it is best to stick with straight edges. If you are not worried about the lack of a hem, you are free to cut the canvas into any shape you like (see the section on No Hem on page 29).

Next, sketch the floorcloth on graph paper, using the lines as guides to draw the shape to scale. Depending on the size of your

This floorcloth was designed to fit the shape and proportions of this kitchen floor. The blue of the cloth accents the tones of the wood and brings color and interest to the room of this horse lover.

floorcloth and the grid of the paper, determine the scale for your drawing. For example, 1 square = 6 inches (15 cm).

Determine the Overall Design

Having chosen a shape and size, you must next decide what kind of design you want to paint on the floorcloth. Go back to your taped layout on the floor. Look around the space. Is there a definitive style throughout the room? Is it a country kitchen, a funky bathroom, or a hallway in a colonial-style house? Is there a specific element that you would like to accentuate or use as a part of the design? This could be anything from a fleur-de-lis from your wallpaper, a tree in a nearby painting, or the shape of a window or door.

Try to imagine seeing the room for the first time. What catches your eye first? What do you dislike about the space? What do you want to highlight? Considering all of these components will help you come up with a design that strengthens the overall feel of the room and accentuates your favorite details.

When planning your floorcloth, keep in mind that size plays a critical role in design. For instance, complex, intricately detailed painting may be lost on a very large

floorcloth. On the other hand, a bold, geometric pattern of very large shapes may overpower a small piece.

On a small floorcloth — one that is less than 3 feet by 4½ feet (90 cm by 135 cm) — detailed, pictorial images are very effective. If you enjoy painting and feel confident using painterly techniques, you can work as you would on any canvas. Just cover the floorcloth with free-flowing applications of paint. Perhaps you'll want to go outside and sketch some ideas from nature or pore over art books to gather specific elements for your floorcloth design. Clip art is readily available through bookstores or the Internet and can be useful for representing a particular object or an animal. You can also repeat a motif to create a nice pattern. If you want to use a geometric pattern on a smaller floorcloth, keep the scale relatively small.

For larger floorcloths, think on a larger scale. These pieces are great for overall geometric and patterned designs. A bolder look can also be achieved by using large blocks of color. Notice that fabric and wallpaper designs are created through the repetition of distinct elements. Use this same technique for large floorcloth designs.

The loosely painted stripes on this floorcloth make a great design for a hallway runner, because they lead the eye through the length of the space.

Tiles can provide inspiration for designs.

Creating Patterns

If you have decided to make a floor-cloth with an overall repeating pattern, you need to make some choices regarding the decorative style, scale of the pattern, and color palette. Repeating patterns are generally geometric in nature.

Alternating, interlocking, and rhythmic placements of shapes stem from a basic mathematical division of the design space. Some may look extremely complicated at first glance but, upon closer examination, are seen to be broken down into manageable sections. In fact, some of the most interesting patterns begin by accident and seem to grow like crystals, becoming a fascinating design all on their own.

You need only one strong motif to build a decorative scheme through repetition, careful placement, and attention to scale. If you want to use pictorial images, try placing spot illustrations in designated areas around the floorcloth, or focus the viewer's attention on a central illustration by painting the surrounding areas in solid colors to guide the eye to a "resting" place.

It also helps to look through magazines and carpet catalogs to get a sense of how scale works on the floor. Keep a spare drawer or a box to store clippings, photographs, and your own sketches to use as guides or inspiration.

One of the most basic floorcloth designs consists of a solid-colored square with a border of a couple of bands of color. The simplicity of this design makes it great under a table or in a small, uncluttered room. It can also be very effective on a larger floorcloth. Add a design motif in each corner to generate more interest. Use some of the textural painting techniques discussed in chapter 6 to create more visual depth.

This pattern was inspired by the diagonal placement of tiles.

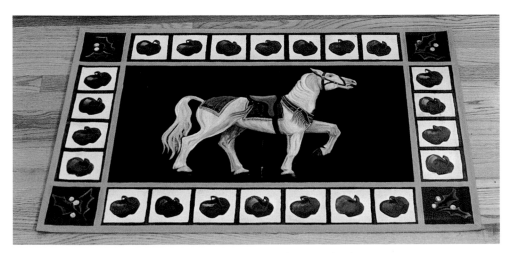

A few repeating elements in a pleasing arrangement can make a complex design.

Pay attention to the scale of the design when you are laying out a plain bordered floorcloth. The larger the floorcloth, the larger the border should be. A border that is too narrow will look undefined. On the other hand, a wide border on a small floorcloth will look more like a striped design than a solid color encompassed by a boundary. Generally speaking, on floorcloths that are smaller than 3 feet by 6 feet (1 m by 2 m), you should keep the border to less than 8 inches (20 cm) wide. On large floorcloths, you can make the border wider than or equal to 8 inches (20 cm).

You can create more complex patterns by taking a few defined elements and laying them out like puzzle pieces until they make a pleasing arrangement. Once you work out the scale and the color palette (more on this topic in chapter 5), you've created a repeating floorcloth pattern.

Complex patterns can also be obtained by using several colors, textural painting techniques, or more design elements, or by making the floorcloth an unusual shape, such as an octagon, an oblong, or a unique outline.

However, be careful not to let all of these fun and playful elements get away from you, or you'll end up with an overly busy floorcloth. Carefully planning the design first on paper can help prevent this from happening.

TESSELLATING PATTERNS

M. C. Escher (1898–1972), the master of tessellating patterns, said, "[A] mental image is something completely different from a visual image, and however much one exerts oneself, one can never manage to capture the fullness of that perfection which hovers in the mind and which one thinks of, quite falsely, as something that is 'seen.' After a long series of attempts, I manage to cast my lovely dream in the defective visual mould of a detailed conceptual sketch. After this, to my great relief, there dawns the second phase, that is the making of the graphic print; for now the spirit can take its rest while the work is taken over by the hands." (Design by Lisa Curry Mair.)

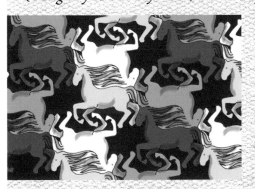

Quilt patterns, such as Morning Star (top) and Fox and Geese (bottom), can inspire your design ideas.

Sources of Inspiration

Where do you come up with the defined elements needed to make a repeating pattern? The sources of inspiration are endless. Nature provides us with leaves, crystalline frost designs on windows, even clouds in the sky. History has given us mosaics, ceramics, fine art, tapestries, and countless architectural gems with fantastic styles of arches, columns, and stonework.

I love to use quilt patterns; they work very well for floorcloths, as they are often made in a similar size and are intended to add an element of decoration to a room rather than to overpower it. Amish quilt patterns are powerful because of their simplicity. Other early American quilt patterns, such as Morning Star and Fox and Geese (at left), are among my favorites because they repeat a simple shape.

I also like to look through wallpaper books as another source for repeated design patterns. You can look through books at the paint store and ask to bring home ones that have designs that appeal to you. You can then trace the parts of the designs that you like and enlarge or reduce them on a photocopier or computer. The added benefit of using wallpaper for ideas is that most sample books usually show several different color combinations, as well.

There are also source books on tile designs, parquet flooring, carpets, and linoleum and vinyl patterns. Any of these books can provide you with a starting point for your own designs. Then, simply expand the pattern and map out a drawing of your floorcloth on graph paper.

Reproducing Design Motifs

When you find a motif that you would like to use as a part of a pattern, you can use several methods to reproduce it onto a floorcloth. Necessity is the mother of invention. It is a tedious study in extreme patience (and the end results are not so interesting, either) to trace a specific motif over and over again, only to force yourself to fill in the lines and paint the design afterward.

Try the following methods, and then use your imagination and inventiveness to develop your own printing or transferring technique.

USING A COMPUTER TO CREATE PATTERNS

If you have access to a computer drawing program, you can create wonderful patterns with just a few clicks of the mouse. Scan or draw the motif into a new file. Stretch, flip, rotate, and transform it using whichever edit commands you want. The trick is to try all kinds of permutations. Save all the results that you like and trash the ones you don't.

When you've got the motif just as you want it, select it, copy it, and paste it in layers so that you can move all the pieces around and try out a variety of compositions. With the "show grid" option turned on, place the copied motifs accurately and evenly on the floor-cloth template. Copy several motifs to form a row, select the row, and then copy and paste multiple rows to form the overall pattern.

This floorcloth, which hangs in the entryway to my studio, is based on an Early American quilt motif.

Stencils

Stencils can be as simple as a heart or as complex as an entire alphabet. The one limitation is the inability to cut out a "floating" detail within a larger shape. Think of a doughnut hole. The only satisfactory way to represent the doughnut with a stencil is to attach the part of the stencil that creates the hole to the outer edges of the stencil with a thin tab. Keep this in mind when working up a stencil design.

MATERIALS

- Graph paper
- Paper
- Acetate, mylar, specialty stencil sheet, or oiled stencil card
- Tape
- Pencil
- Transfer paper
- Cutting board or folded newspaper
- Craft knife

1. To create a stencil, first work out the best size for the motif. Draw the entire floorcloth design on graph paper. Count the number of squares incorporated by the design and multiply this number by the scale on the graph paper to calculate the actual size of the motif. Enlarge the motif on paper to the desired size (a).

2. Make a stencil from a sheet of acetate or Mylar, a specialty stencil sheet, or an oiled stencil card that is at least 2 inches (5 cm) larger in each direction than the motif. If you use a relatively clear stencil sheet, such as mylar or acetate, tape the design on the back and trace it with a pencil. Since acetate cracks and tears easily, be careful cutting and washing the stencil to avoid losing intricate pieces of the design. If you use a specialty stencil sheet or an oiled stencil card, transfer the motif with carbon paper and a pencil.

3. Place the stencil sheet or card on a cutting board or a piece of folded newspaper. Place the stencil

on top of the design. Using a small craft knife with a sharp blade (change it often for best results), carefully cut out the design (b).

Use stencil cream to paint the design (c). You can also buy pre-cut stencils at craft, art supply, hardware, and decorating supply stores or order them through specialty shops or the Internet.

CARING FOR YOUR STENCILS

Stencils can be used over and over again. If you are using water-soluble stencil cream, wash the stencil with warm, soapy water. Be careful not to scrub too hard, as scrubbing can break intricate stencil details. Clean stencil brushes by putting a dab of dish soap in the palm of your hand and rubbing the brush in a circular motion to work the soap into the bristles. Rinse it in warm water, still rubbing the bristles in the palm of your hand, until the water runs completely clear.

Graduated Stencils

A more complex stenciling method involves using two or more colors that bleed into each other as you move down the design. In this case, you'll need only one stencil but several colors of paint and a stencil brush for each color.

For this technique, stencil cream is the easiest paint to use. It is not runny, as latex house paint is, and therefore will not seep under the stencil and cause irregular edges. Stencil brushes are usually fairly stiff and have a flat, round surface. Rub the brush into the stencil cream, and then test-paint a small piece of canvas. You need enough paint on the brush to leave a light coat of color when it is rubbed into the canvas. Too much paint will be hard to work with and will bleed out under the stencil. Too little paint will be barely visible.

When you've tried the technique and are happy with the look on your test swatch, apply paint to the stencil. A soft, variegated effect is more pleasing to the eye than a heavy, solid application of color. You can also apply paint by using a sponge, a sponge brush, or a can of spray paint. Experiment with these techniques before trying them on your floorcloth.

Layered Stencils

Stencils with multiple overlays are used to create dimension and to paint designs with more than one color. Art supply sources sell a large variety of two- and three-layered stencils that have built-in registration marks. Three-dimensional effects can be achieved by stenciling with a medium tone, a highlight, and a shadow. Let the paint dry between applications.

If you cut your own stencils, it's important to make registration lines on each stencil, so that you can line them up correctly. Draw one vertical line and one horizontal line at right angles to each other with a permanent marker on each stencil. Next, carefully draw guidelines on the canvas using watercolor pencils.

Above, a commercial stencil shows the layers of ochre and rust paint used to create a textural effect on canvas, top right. A leaf pattern, right, is created with three stencils in the steps below.

These lines help you place the stencil accurately, so that the pattern is spaced correctly from one stencil to the next. Align the registration lines on the stencil with the guidelines on the canvas and fix the stencil in place with a few small pieces of tape.

1. Tape the corners of the first stencil to the canvas beneath. Apply paint to layer #1 and allow to dry.

2. Lining up the registration marks, tape the corners of the second stencil in the same place as the first one. Apply paint and let dry.

3. Tape the third stencil in the same place and paint the final layer of the design.

Stamps

Stamps are fun to make and extremely durable. Very intricate designs that can be successfully cut in stencil sheets, though, are harder to replicate on a stamp. However, with some care, you can create complex motifs.

MATERIALS

- Paper template
- Craft knife
- Art foam sheets 1/16 in. to 1/8 in. thick (1.5 mm to 3 mm)
- Repositionable adhesive
- Ballpoint pen or permanent marker
- Sharp craft scissors
- Styrofoam blue board (available at hardware stores)
- White glue

1. Make a paper template of the motif and number each part of the design. Use a craft knife to cut out the design.

2. Spray the art foam sheet lightly with repositionable adhesive. Place the paper template on the foam sheet. Trace the positive spaces using a ballpoint pen or permanent marker. Number each element, matching the numbers on the template.

3. With sharp craft scissors, cut out all of the shapes. Lift the template from the foam, being careful not to tear the paper.

4. Position the negative template on the blue board. Trace the motif again and number the elements. Now you are ready to put the pieces together. Match all the numbers and glue each piece into its appropriate place on the blue board. Use a thin layer of white glue, and wipe up any glue that seeps out from under the foam. While the glue is wet, adjust all of the pieces so that they line up well and the design is accurate. Allow the stamp to dry at least overnight.

Customized stamps are easy to make with a few simple materials. Trace a chosen design, cut it out with scissors, use the pieces as a template to cut identical shapes out of art foam, then position the foam pieces on blue board.

Enlarging and Transferring Designs

Once you have worked out an entire design on graph paper (or in a drawing or painting program on your computer), you are ready to transfer the image to a blank floorcloth.

- Watercolor pencils
- Prepared canvas floorcloth
- Photocopier or computer (if using step 3)
- Small-scale graph paper and plain paper (if using step 4)
- Newsprint or large sheet of paper
- Tape
- Transfer paper
- Ballpoint pen

1. If you are using a border, draw a line with watercolor pencil around the perimeter of the floorcloth to indicate the entire border, including smaller accent lines or repeating detail elements of the border itself. (The pencil lines can be erased later with a wet paintbrush and a paper towel.)

2. Identify the main elements of your pattern to transfer first. Draw light watercolor pencil lines to use as guides for placing stencil, stamps, or other repeating design elements.

3. Enlarge any repeating elements to fit within the lined spaces. You can use a photocopier to enlarge up to 11 inches by 17 inches on office copiers, but it will be hit or miss to find the exact measurement you need. A better route is to use a computer. With the "view rulers" or "show grids" options on, enlarge the motif to fit the specified space. Click "print," and you have a template that is ready to use.

   Alternate option: Another way to enlarge your design and make a template is to trace the motif onto small-scale graph paper. On another sheet of paper that is at least the size of your motif, draw grid lines to represent the graph paper in the enlarged scale you need. For example, suppose you have sketched a 2-inch-square (5 cm) motif on ¼-inch (.625 cm) graph paper and the motif needs to be 8 inches (20 cm) square on the floorcloth. You'll need to draw grid lines in 1-inch (2.5 cm) increments on the sheet of paper. Next, use the squares of the graph paper as guides to transfer the image to the larger grid. Mark where lines cross the gridlines and connect these marks.

To transfer a freehand drawing onto your floorcloth, draw it first at full scale on newsprint or some other large sheet of paper. Draw a vertical and a horizontal line through the center of the design. These are your positioning lines. With watercolor pencil, draw similar lines on your floorcloth, extending them all the way to the edges.

4. Center the template (the photocopied enlargement, the computer printout, or the newsprint drawing) on the floorcloth, matching the positioning lines carefully, and tape it down along one side. Slide a sheet of transfer paper under the design and

firmly draw over it with a ballpoint pen to transfer the image to the floorcloth. You will need to use either light or dark transfer paper, depending on the background color of the floorcloth, so that the transferred design shows clearly.

Enlarging and transferring a freehand drawing

TROMPE L'OEIL

If a frame works for a painting on the wall, why not make it work for a painting on the floor? Paint a border to look like wood. Add graining, carved details, and miter marks in the corners to make it even more realistic. A picket or post-and-rail fence is another interesting option. For a real trompe l'oeil effect, try painting a small stone wall or a hedge to contain the design. This floorcloth by Alan Vaughn looks like cracked tile. (Photograph by Alan Vaughn.)

Designing Borders

A border serves to contain the design by defining itself as separate from the rest of the floorcloth. A distinct change in the pattern's color, tone, or scale works well to indicate where the main design ends and the border begins. Think of the border as a visual stop. It leads the eye around the design, following the pattern and the color, and then guides the eye to the edge, where it quietly comes to rest.

Without a border, many designs seem to fall off the edge of the floorcloth; the viewer may have a sense of being left dangling. This feeling of suspension is accentuated when the floorcloth is put on the floor. People like to feel that they are standing on firm ground! Look at the masterful patterns on oriental rugs. Invariably, these rugs make

good use of borders, some of which are extremely intricate.

On smaller floorcloths — those less than 3 feet by 4½ feet (90 cm by 135 cm) — the border can be as simple as a solid line and as narrow as ½ inch (1 cm) in a coordinating or contrasting color. Consider how a frame placed on a finished piece of artwork changes the entire look of the painting.

Some framing specialists will tell you that the frame is more important than the artwork. This may not be true, but certainly the frame — or, in this case, the border — greatly influences the way the floorcloth is perceived. If your floorcloth shows a scene or a portrait, a border will improve the overall composition.

As the floorcloth becomes larger, the size of the border should increase proportionately. In general, the border should be at least half the

width of the main repeating design elements. Smaller details can be incorporated within the border, as well, but remember to end the pattern with a visual stop, or a solid line around the outermost edge.

For floorcloths that will be used under kitchen or dining room tables, an effective design may include a textured pattern stamped lightly in the center and surrounded by a lively, colorful border. This is because the table and chairs will cover the center area of the floorcloth, leaving the border as the focal point.

The reverse is true for floorcloths that will fill an area and have furniture placed around the perimeter. In those cases, the border dwindles in significance in relation to the interior space. Therefore, the border should be simpler than the central design.

Incorporating Designs into Borders

You may want to integrate the interior design with the border design by repeating key elements in both places. For instance, consider painting a central clump of grapes on a dark background and define it with a separating line. Then encircle the design with a border of vines with clumps of grapes in the corners painted on the same dark background and wrapped in the same separating line. Check historical sources for all kinds of central medallion ideas.

WRAPAROUND WORDS

For an interesting border effect, try placing words or letters around the perimeter of a floorcloth. You can use famous quotes, your own poetic prose, or the alphabet wrapped around a design. If painted in a color that barely contrasts with the background, the words become a sort of secret surprise for observant visitors. Or paint the words big and bold to make a real statement.

Intricate borders, such as the ones pictured below and on facing page, frame a simpler interior pattern and make a striking design that draws the eye to the edges of the floorcloth.

Flowers and Sprigs

6 feet x 6 feet (180 cm x 180 cm)

This design, with its sunny display of flowers on a soft background and a running border of leaves, is perfect for a sunroom or other cheerful, open space. The botanical element of blossoms and greens creates a natural, relaxed feel. The flowers establish the rhythm of the pattern, which is elaborated with vibrant colors. The size of the sprigs and lines that make up the border is related to the size of the flowers. The square shape of the floorcloth itself is echoed in the squares at the corners of the border. Each of these seemingly small details adds up to a strong design.

MATERIALS

- Prepared canvas, 6 ft. x 6 ft.
- 1 qt. (1 liter) *each* flat finish latex paint, colors #1, #2, and #3
- Small decorator's paint brush
- Index card
- 4-in. (10 cm) house painter's brush
- HB pencil
- Ruler
- Flowers and Sprigs template
- Watercolor pencils
- Flower Stencil template
- 10-in. (25 cm) stencil sheet (mylar, acetate, or oiled card)
- Sharp craft knife
- Stencil brush
- 2 oz. (60 ml) tube acrylic paint or stencil cream, color #4
- 2 oz. (60 ml) *each* tube acrylic paint, colors #5, #6, and #7
- Small flat watercolor brush
- Sprig Stamp template
- 5 in. x 10 in. (12.5 cm x 25 cm) piece of ⅛-in. (3 mm) art foam
- 5 in. x 10 in. (12.5 cm x 25 cm) piece of 1-in. (2.5 cm) blue board
- 1-in. (2.5 cm) sponge brush
- Water
- Paper towels
- 1 gal. (3.785 liter) water-based polyurethane, semigloss finish
- 1 qt. (1 liter) water-based polyurethane, satin finish

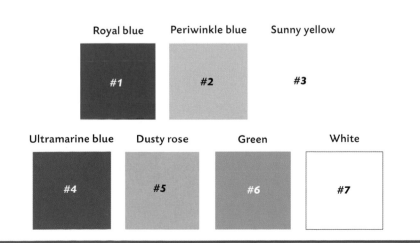

COLOR CHOICES

Use these colors or select your own combination using the code below. Names of paint colors vary from brand to brand, so I won't use specific color names. Simply take this book to the paint store and match the swatches.

Royal blue	Periwinkle blue	Sunny yellow
#1	#2	#3

Ultramarine blue	Dusty rose	Green	White
#4	#5	#6	#7

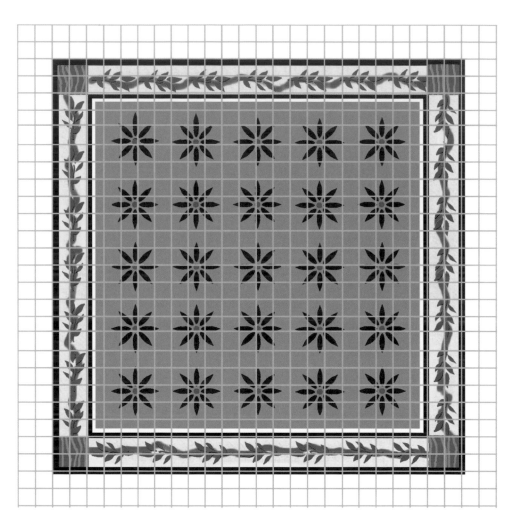

Flowers and Sprigs Template
1 square = 3" (7.5 cm)

Prepare the Floorcloth

1. Paint the back hem of the floor-cloth using color #1 and the small decorator's paint brush. Slide the index card along under the hem to prevent painting the back of the floorcloth.

2. Turn the floorcloth over and paint the front using color #2 and the 4-inch (10 cm) house painter's brush. Allow the floorcloth to dry overnight.

3. With the HB pencil and a ruler, draw the line for the border 7 inches (17.5 cm) in from the outer edge of the floorcloth. Paint the background of the border with two coats of color #3 and the small decorator's brush. Allow the border to dry after each coat is applied.

Stencil the Flowers

1. Using the Flowers and Sprigs Template on the facing page, make stencil guidelines using the watercolor pencils (see page 131 for a larger template you can photocopy).

2. Using the template for the Flower Stencil (right), cut the stencil sheet with a sharp craft knife as described on page 39. Lay the stencil on the floorcloth and align it with the penciled guidelines. Secure it with a few small pieces of masking tape.

3. Stencil the flowers with the stencil brush. For the flower petals, use acrylic paint or stencil cream in color #4; for the flower centers, use color #5. Lift the stencil and carefully reposition it in the next section of the grid. Repeat this until 25 flowers have been stenciled onto the floorcloth.

4. Paint a thin, wavy line with a small, flat watercolor brush and color #5, thinned to allow easy, free-flowing brush strokes.

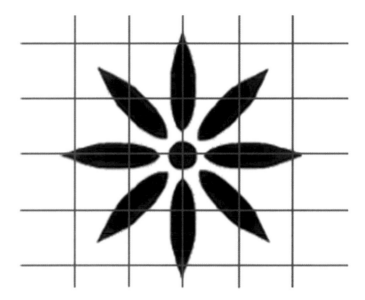

Flower Stencil
1 square = 2" (5 cm)

Stenciling the flowers

Stamp the Sprigs

1. Using the template for the Sprig Stamp (below right), prepare the stamp with the art foam and blue board as described on page 42.

2. Paint color #6 onto the stamp with the sponge brush. Align the stamp on the border and press it firmly to transfer the image onto the floorcloth. Lift the stamp, reload it with paint, and continue stamping until the whole border is completed.

3. Paint the corner squares color #5, let dry, and add stripes in color #2.

Finish the Floorcloth

1. When the floorcloth is completely dry, use the HB pencil to draw the inner and outer lines for the border. Paint the border color #1 with an inner line of color #7. Allow the floorcloth to dry overnight.

2. Use a small decorator's brush and water to erase the watercolor pencil lines. Rub the water into the lines and dab the surface with a paper towel to lift the color from the floorcloth.

Stamping the sprigs

3. Use the house painter's brush to apply 3 coats of semigloss polyurethane for normal traffic (4 coats for rougher use). Allow at least 8 hours of drying time in between coats.

4. Apply a final coat of satin polyurethane using the house painter's brush. Allow the floorcloth to cure for at least a week before you put it on the floor.

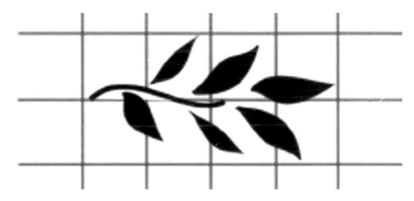

Sprig Stamp
1 square = 2" (5 cm)

VARIATIONS ON A THEME

For alternative designs, you can incorporate the same flower motifs but vary the border, the choice of colors, and the play of light and dark. Experiment with a different type of border or make a wider or narrower frame around the central pattern. Sketch the design, and then cut the border away with scissors and paste on variations.

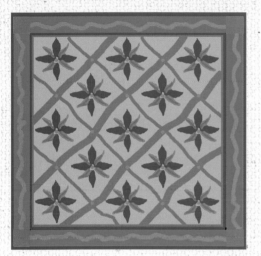

Flowers and Stripes
6 feet x 6 feet (180 cm x 180 cm)

The flowers on this floorcloth are painted freehand; loose stripes add definition and interest. To make this design, paint the background periwinkle with bold, loose stripes of magenta on top. Paint the flowers with large, free strokes and add green secondary petals. Large rose dots scattered evenly over the surface and a squiggly stripe on the green border create a cheerful, relaxed pattern. Seal the floorcloth with polyurethane.

Home Sweet Home
6 feet x 6 feet (180 cm x 180 cm)

Since words encircle this border, viewers must be able to see the floorcloth from all sides. The best place for a floorcloth with this type of border is in the center of a room with traffic flowing in all directions. To create the letters, you can use stencils or paint them in your own script. If you want to sketch the words freehand, draw guidelines in watercolor pencil first, and then center the letters and words before painting them. You can also type the words on a computer, enlarge them on a photocopier, tape them to the border, and then trace them with carbon paper. Carefully paint the letters using a fine, liner brush. Seal the floorcloth with polyurethane.

Flowers and Spirals Runner
2 feet x 6 feet (60 cm x 180 cm)

This floorcloth has a basic striped border with splashes of freehand spirals and large, stenciled or freehand flowers in contrasting but coordinating colors. Play with this design by selecting different colors or changing the scale of the flowers, center dots, and spirals. Spontaneous additions often create a spark that is never the same when planned. To make this floorcloth, paint the background green and the border rose. Paint the royal-blue border stripes before applying the flowers in sunny yellow using the flower stencil. Paint the 8-inch-diameter spiral shapes ivory and the flower and spiral centers rose. Seal the floorcloth with polyurethane.

Combining Colors

CHOOSING THE COLORS for your floorcloth is a fun and fascinating part of the design process. Using a computer with a drawing program, colored pencils or markers, or paint chips from the hardware store, you can try out endless color possibilities for even the simplest design. The tricky part is deciding which color combination best suits your taste and décor.

This chapter will help you understand how colors play off each other to create a sense of calm, vibrancy, coolness, warmth, or whatever you prefer. The color wheel is a tool that will help you select colors for your floorcloth. Tips for selecting a color palette will also help you get started. Armed with a little bit of theory and a lot of imagination, you can create beautiful color combinations that will enhance any room.

Floorcloths by Orbo Design (photograph by Beth Schneckenburger).

Some Definitions

Primary Colors: Red, yellow, and blue

Secondary Colors: Orange, green, and purple

Complementary Colors: Colors directly opposite each other on the color wheel (red and green, yellow and purple, blue and orange)

Monochromatic Colors: Variations of a single hue that differ only in tone or intensity (such as shades of blue)

Hue: The actual color of a pigment

Intensity or **Saturation:** Brightness or chromatic purity (the amount of white, black, or gray)

Tone or **Value:** The lightness or darkness of a color

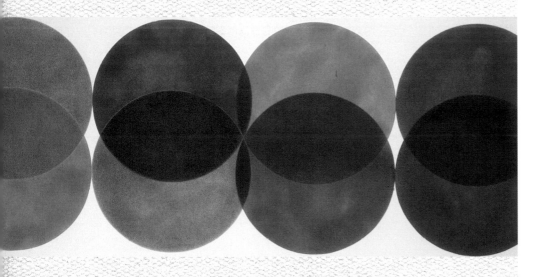

Color Theory

Color can have an enormous impact on a room. While color choice is highly personal, it can make the difference between a cozy or a dynamic space, between a cheerful or a relaxing room. Being familiar with a few basic color terms and theoretical concepts will help you make an effective floorcloth design for your space. For a more comprehensive discussion on color and the emotional, psychological, and aesthetic effects it has on us, consult painting, interior decorating, and graphic arts books and magazines.

Three basic dimensions define a color: hue, intensity, and tone. When you look at a color chip, the basic color — red, green, yellow, or blue — is called the *hue*. Is it electric pink or shell pink? That is the *intensity*. The *tone* is the lightness or darkness of the color.

Orbo Design has acheived the effect of translucence in this section of a floorcloth by layering colors to create overlapping circles. It is a study in intensity and hue. The value of each color has been carefully selected to create a vivid new color in the overlapped area of each set of circles.

Intensity is determined by the brightness of colors. Above, vibrant hues create a visual feast that dominate a room. (Floorcloth and photograph by Linda Arthurs.)

EXERCISE YOUR COLOR MUSCLES

Look around the room you are in and pick out a solid-colored object. Describe it in terms of its hue, intensity, and tone. Now see if you can find something that is the same hue but a different intensity, and then something else that is the same hue but a different tone. Now the harder part. See if you can find something else with the same intensity and tone but a different hue. This exercise is helpful, because later you will play with how related colors work together.

Warm and Cool Colors

All colors can be grouped into one of two categories: warm or cool. Think of summer's sultry reds, oranges, and yellows; these are warm colors. Warm colors are "advancing" colors — they appear to move toward the viewer. Now think of winter's icy blues; these are cool colors. Cool colors are "receding" colors — they create the appearance of moving away from the viewer.

A color can also be perceived as warm or cool depending on the colors surrounding it. For instance, light green and violet fall between the warm and the cool ranges and can be perceived as either warm or cool depending on the other hues around them. In addition, you can warm up a color by adding yellow or red to it, or cool it down by mixing it with blue.

Since warm colors create a sense of closeness and cool colors promote a sense of distance, you can combine colors to create depth within a painting or in a room. For example, bright yellow sunflowers on a light blue background will pop toward the viewer. Juxtaposing colors in this way adds depth and dimension and creates a sense of space on a flat surface, enhancing the optical illusion of the painting.

Cool, watery depths are evoked by both the color choice and the subject matter in the work at right. (Floorcloth and photograph by Pamela Marwede.)

Warmth radiates from the colors and motif in the example above.
(Floorcloth by Susan Arnold, photograph by G. B. Hubbard.)

purple on a lighter color

purple on a darker color

purple on its complement

purple on a similar value color

purple on white

How Surrounding Hues Affect Color

Color does not exist in a vacuum but is affected by the other colors around it. For instance, purple (in the example at left) appears darker when the colors around it are lighter. Conversely, it appears lighter when surrounded by darker colors. In addition, it appears to be a different color when it is surrounded by its complementary color, yellow.

Be careful when placing two complementary colors right next to each other — if they are equal in tone they will not harmonize well but will create a sense of vibration that can be unpleasant to the eye. Two complementary colors placed next to each other are more pleasing when they have different tones.

The pattern and rhythm of a design are formed, in part, by such tonal contrasts. Think of a checkerboard design. The only element affecting that pattern is the play of total opposites in tone — pure black and pure white. The intensity of the colors provides the overall feel of the piece. A few splashes of a brilliant color can spice up an otherwise dull pattern, or an overall vivid display of bright, vibrant hues can make a bold, contemporary design. A color scheme made up of consistently muted colors can provide a sense of warmth.

This floorcloth uses carefully chosen surrounding colors to create subtle effects. The thin red stripe around the yellow center adds depth to an already warm hue. The cool yellow stripe surrounding the deep green square looks especially vivid sandwiched between warm colors. (Floorcloth by Orbo Design, photograph by Beth Schneckenburger.)

How Light Affects Color

Light has an enormous impact on color. The position of the sun affects color and can change how a color appears throughout the day. Bright, natural light makes colors look lighter than they really are. On the other hand, dim light makes colors appear darker. Electric lighting also has important effects. Incandescent light produces a warm, yellowish cast, while fluorescent light produces a white or bluish cast, which tends to reduce a color's warmth.

Before you make any major decisions about the color palette for a floorcloth, test out small color swatches in the room in which you plan to use it. Look at the swatches at various times of day as well as at night. A color that looks pleasing in natural light may not be as attractive at night with overhead lights and lamps turned on (the reverse may also be true). Test color swatches in various places in the room, as the angle at which the sun enters affects color in different locations.

The bright sunlight in this room makes the floorcloth colors look lighter than they actually are. The size, shape, and colors of this piece were chosen so that the floorcloth would be the focal point of this space.

THE COLOR WHEEL

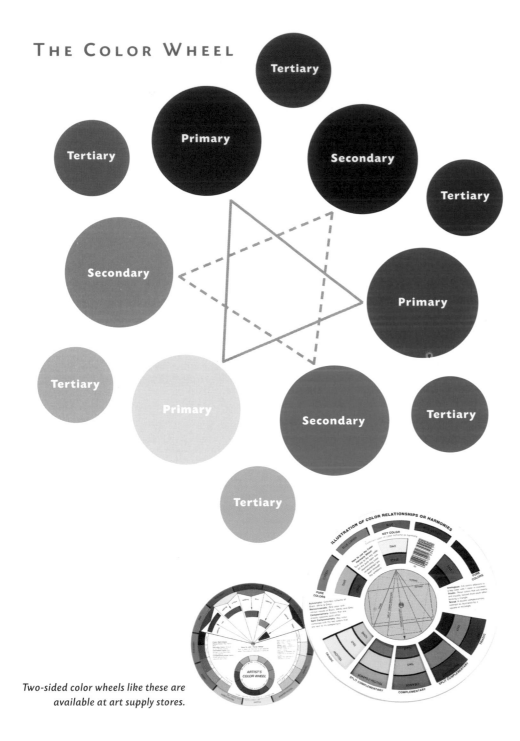

Two-sided color wheels like these are available at art supply stores.

The Color Wheel

The color wheel is a tool that is used by many artists. All of the colors of the rainbow are placed around the perimeter of the wheel with the primary colors of red, yellow, and blue equidistant from each other. The three colors in between — orange, green, and purple — are each a blend of the two primary colors adjacent to it (red and yellow make orange, for example). Tertiary colors are created by blending each primary color with the secondary color beside it (red and purple, for example, make magenta).

You can purchase various types of color wheels in art supply stores. Color wheels often have three inner rings. The outermost ring is painted at full intensity. The middle ring contains the same colors, but they are dulled slightly with a small amount of each color's complement and an equal amount of white. The innermost ring is made up of the same colors darkened with a little black. This forms a complete scale of hue, intensity, and tone.

You can use a color wheel to choose colors that evoke a mood.

Hot colors, such as red, are strong and stimulating, while cold colors, such as blue, are calming. Warm colors have a yellow tone that is considered comforting. Cool colors, which have a blue tone, are soothing and refreshing. Very light colors, such as white and faint pastels, can evoke a sense of spaciousness and airiness. Dark, somber hues, including black and brown, tend to seem serious and focused. Pale, soft colors, which contain predominantly white pigment, are considered gentle and romantic. Bright, bold colors can be cheerful and exhilarating.

The color wheel can also help you select a color range that is pleasing to your eye. For instance, a harmonic range contains colors that are next to each other on the color wheel plus one complementary color. Such a palette is subtle and creates a sense of symmetry. A melodic range contains two or more tones of the same hue plus black and white. This palette produces a more monochromatic color scheme. Introducing a dissonant color — a shade on the opposite side of the color wheel — creates contrast and drama.

Colors of similar intensity enhanced by soft, curving shapes create a charming composition in the example above. Note that contrasting colors used in this way can have a muted effect. (Floorcloth by Linda Locke, photograph by Dan Delaney.)

High-contrast colors and jagged, powerful shapes create an invigorating effect in the piece above. (Floorcloth by Natalie Browne-Gutnik, photograph by F. Fisher.)

Similar palettes of reds and greens can look very different, depending on the style, pattern, and composition of the piece.

Above, red provides a vivid background for a folk-art style composition. (Floorcloth and photograph by Mary Lou Keith.)

Near right, a small amount of green provides visual relief and punch on a monochromatic red background. (Floorcloth by Natalie Browne-Gutnik, photograph by F. Fisher.)

Far right, a trompe l'oeil design in shades of red, green, and yellow creates a high-impact composition. (Floorcloth and photograph by Skip Dyrda.)

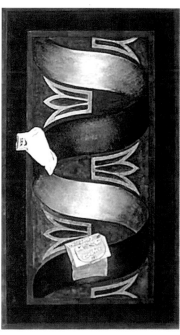

Selecting a Color Palette

You can select a color palette for your floorcloth that blends with the wall color and furnishings in a room, or choose a palette that provides contrast to an existing color scheme. You can also select a color palette that reflects a particular design scheme, such as contemporary, country, or traditional, or one that picks up a pattern and color scheme in a fabric or wall covering.

FIVE STEPS TO SELECTING THE PERFECT PALETTE

To select a palette, try following these steps:

1. Look at the significant colors in the room where the floorcloth will go.

2. Decide what results you want to achieve with color. Do you want the room to feel intimate, airy, spacious, relaxing, or vibrant? Do you want to distract the eye from a feature you don't like or enhance an architectural detail?

3. Gather color samples from the room by snipping off fabric from underneath a chair or inside a slipcover. Go to the paint store and select color chips that match, blend with, or contrast with those colors.

4. Select a main color and a palette based on that color.

5. Refine the colors by changing the tone or intensity to achieve the exact tints or shades you want.

Colored pencils and tracing paper can be helpful tools when experimenting with color combinations. Draw your floorcloth on the paper and then place it over a photograph of the room where the floorcloth will reside to see how the colors coordinate with the décor.

Color Inspiration

Nearly anything can inspire a color palette — nature, great works of art, existing fabric and wallpaper in a room. You can even paint a floorcloth to match your sofa!

If you want to design a floorcloth to match a room, it's useful to make what interior designers refer to as a *storyboard,* or a collection of all the color and design elements in the room. This helps you see the colors and patterns next to each other in an organized fashion that isn't overwhelming. It also focuses your visual perceptions, which stimulates design ideas.

For example, the living room featured on the facing page was wallpapered with two coordinating papers, and the sofa and pillows were upholstered in closely matching fabrics. The chocolate brown of one of the pillows was chosen for the center of the floorcloth; the border echoes the beige paint on the wood trim in the room. The design was stenciled in the same soft celery green that is an accent in the wallpaper. The design does not match the fabric and wallpaper in any way, but it utilizes the same colors effectively. The result: The floorcloth unifies the room. *(Floorcloth by Janet Harris.)*

Freehand Plaid

2½ feet x 5 feet (75 cm x 150 cm)

This design, with its blocks of color and loosely painted stripes and zig-zags, is fun to have underfoot in all kinds of living spaces. The colors I have used create a warm, Southwestern feel, but you can change the combinations to create a cheerful Mediterranean rug or a funky retro look (see Variations on a Theme on page 71).

(see Variations on a Theme on page 71)

MATERIALS

- Prepared canvas, 30 in. x 60 in.
- 1 cup (240 ml) *each* flat finish latex paint, colors #1, #2, and #3
- Small decorator's paintbrush
- 4-in. (10 cm) house painter's brush
- Freehand Plaid template
- Pencil
- Small plastic container
- Water
- 2 oz. (60 ml) *each* tube acrylic paint, colors #4 and #5
- ½-in. (1 cm) flat brush
- 1-in. (2.5 cm) flat brush
- 1 qt. (1 liter) polyurethane, semigloss finish
- 1 qt. (1 liter) polyurethane, satin finish

COLOR CHOICES

Use these colors or select your own combination using the code below. Names of colors vary from brand to brand, so I won't use specific names. Simply take this book to the paint store and match the swatches.

Dark teal	Barn red	Pale green	Peach	Ivory
#1	#2	#3	#4	#5

Prepare the Floorcloth

1. Paint the back hem of the floor-cloth color #1 with a small decorator's paintbrush. Allow it to dry thoroughly.

2. Turn the floorcloth over and paint the front color #2, using the house painter's brush. Allow it to dry thoroughly.

3. Using the Freehand Plaid Template below (see page 132 for a larger template you can photocopy) and a pencil, transfer the pattern to the floorcloth. Draw only the lines as indicated on the template to act as guides. This design will be painted using loose (not crisp or measured) lines.

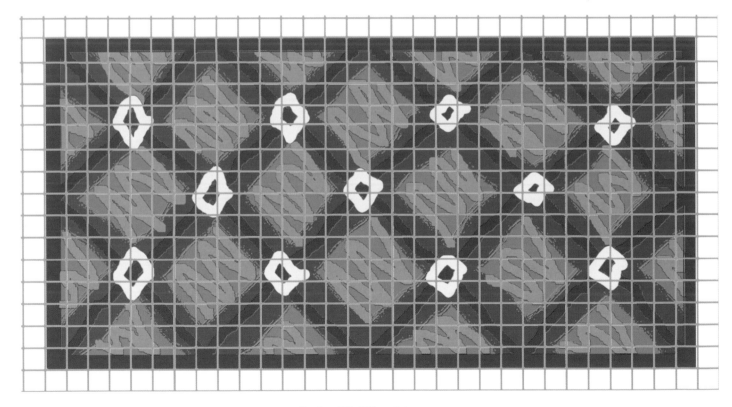

Freehand Plaid Template
1 square = 2" (5 cm)

Paint the Design

1. With the small decorator's brush and color #3, loosely paint 6-inch (15 cm) squares inside the plaid guidelines. Allow the paint to dry thoroughly.

2. In a small plastic container, add enough water to color #4 to allow the paint to flow smoothly. Using the ½-inch (1 cm) flat brush, apply free-flowing zigzags across the color #3 squares. Let them dry.

3. Use color #1 and the 1-inch (2.5 cm) paintbrush to paint the plaid stripes between the squares. Allow the paint to dry thoroughly.

4. Paint the contrasting light squares with color #5 and the ½-inch (1 cm) paintbrush. Let the paint dry.

5. Finish the design by adding a 2-inch (5 cm) border around the entire edge in color #1. Allow the floorcloth to dry overnight.

Finish the Floorcloth

1. With the house painter's brush, apply three coats of semigloss polyurethane for normal traffic (four coats for rougher use). Allow 8 hours of drying time between coats and after the final coat.

2. Apply a final coat of satin polyurethane using the house painter's brush. Allow the floor-cloth to cure for at least a week before putting it on the floor.

VARIATIONS ON A THEME

Revising the colors and/or modifying the pattern for this design can create very different effects.

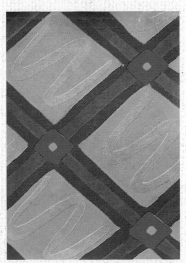

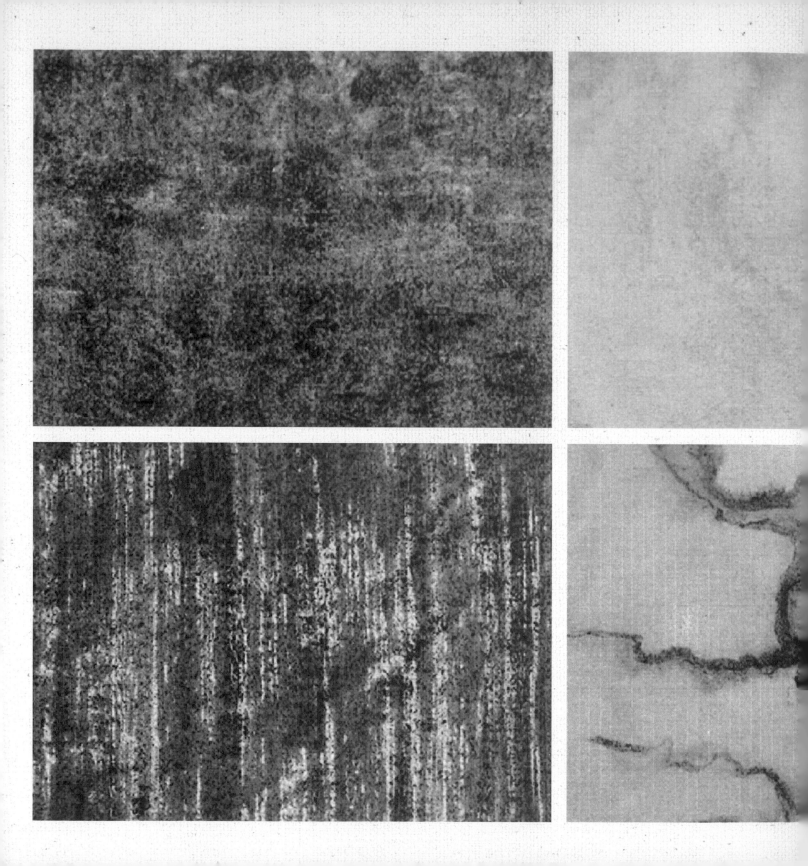

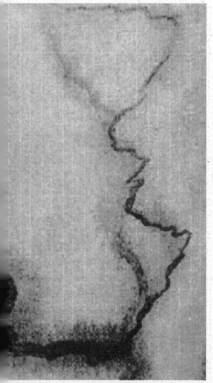

Painting Techniques

HEAVYWEIGHT CANVAS HAS a wonderful natural weave that enables you to produce a wide array of painted effects. A loose wash of color over a dried layer of flat paint can transform a design. Like looking down through a still pond, you see depth and subtle, natural changes in shade, which make the color — and the painted canvas itself — come to life. Sponging and ragging add textural variation, while dragging emphasizes direction and movement.

All of these techniques change the perceived surface of the canvas. With just a few simple tools, you can make a flat blue canvas look like pliable leather or replicate the majestic look of stone, persuade a boring swatch of red to take on the roughness of brick, and make a dull green background appear as soft as moss. A floorcloth painted with several textural techniques, carefully thought out and executed, is a work of art.

Washes

When a thin, watery splash of paint is loosely applied over an existing layer of dry paint, it is called a wash or a glaze. By breaking up a flat space, washes add interest to an otherwise monotonous field of color. When attempting your first washes, try using two colors that differ merely in shade. For example, a wash of teal applied over a flat surface of sea foam blue will create a nice, watery feel. As you become more familiar with colors and how they work together, experiment with more daring combinations.

Materials

- Preshrunk, unpainted canvas
- Latex paint, flat finish
- House painter's brush
- Acrylic paint
- Small glass or plastic container
- 1 tbsp. (15 ml) paint conditioner
- ¼ cup (60 ml) water
- Bucket of water
- 2-in. (5 cm) paintbrush
- Scrap canvas

1. On a preshrunk, unpainted canvas apply a solid color of latex flat-finish paint with a house painter's brush. This is the base coat. Take care to push the paint deep into the weave of the canvas. If you skip spots, the next layer of paint will sink into them and create dark areas. Let the base coat dry thoroughly.

2. Squeeze a dime-size blob of acrylic paint into a small glass or plastic container. Add 1 tablespoon (15 ml) of paint conditioner. The conditioner allows the acrylic to flow smoothly when mixed with water. It also extends the drying time, which lets you work with the entire surface to even out all areas. Add ¼ cup (60 ml) of water and stir thoroughly to create a smooth, cloudy liquid. Most conditioners are cloudy when they are wet and will make the wash look lighter than it will be when it is dry. Always test a small sample on scrap canvas (paper and wood react differently) and let it dry to check for color accuracy before applying the wash to a floorcloth.

3. Fill a bucket with water. With a house painter's brush, paint water over the entire surface. Slap the water on quickly, especially if you are working on a large piece of canvas. When the entire surface is evenly wet and appears shiny, you are ready to apply the wash.

4. Use a paintbrush that is large enough to hold quite a bit of paint, but not so big that you may be tempted to even out the whole surface with too many strokes. If you will be washing 6-inch to 8-inch (15 cm to 20 cm) squares at a time, a 2-inch (5 cm) paintbrush works well.

A loose, confident brush stroke is essential to a terrific wash. First practice making the stroke on scrap canvas. The stroke should have varying weight and a slight wave to create the most interesting effect. As you apply the wash, it will bleed out into the water on the surface of the base coat. You will see it spreading and running in a variety of directions. Don't try too hard to control this. The loose, free-flowing, watery effect is what you're after. And don't panic if it looks too dark. When it dries, the pigment will sink into the canvas and appear less intense.

5. After you apply the wash, the floorcloth will be very wet. It is important not to move the piece until it is dry. If you pick up the canvas, the water (and the carefully applied wash) will run to the lowest point and form a dark puddle. So much for artistic brush strokes. Let the canvas dry overnight. Do not try to speed this process with a hairdryer. The wash will be blown around and, again, the brushstrokes will disappear.

6. Practice with a variety of colors, brush sizes, and amounts of water to see what technique works best for you.

Applying a wash

WORKING ON A FLAT SURFACE

If you've ever tried applying a wash or ragging design on a wall, you've probably noticed how the runny paint is difficult to control.

Applying textural effects on the flat surface of a floorcloth is much easier. Washes stay where they are put, and the weave of the canvas helps contain drips.

Sponging

MATERIALS

- Canvas floorcloth prepared with base coat
- Acrylic paint
- Wide-mouth plastic container
- 1 tbsp. (15 ml) paint extender
- ⅛ cup (30 ml) water
- Scrap canvas
- Latex gloves
- Natural sea sponge
- Bucket of water

Natural sea sponges make interesting textures in paint. Sponging is referred to as a "positive" application — you add color in a haphazard pattern on top of an existing layer of paint. The sponging medium is translucent and slightly thicker than the washes created in the previous section (see pages 74–75). For a guaranteed result, sponge a darker color over a related but lighter base coat. To achieve a richer texture, use different colors of similar intensity.

1. Prepare the canvas floorcloth and apply a base coat. Allow the paint to dry thoroughly.

2. Squeeze a quarter-size blob of acrylic paint into a wide-mouth plastic container and add 1 tablespoon (15 ml) of paint extender. The extender allows the acrylic to flow smoothly when mixed with water. It also extends the drying time, which allows you to continue working with the entire surface to even out all areas. Add ⅛ cup (30 ml) of water and stir thoroughly to create a smooth liquid. Always test a small sample on scrap canvas and allow it to dry to check for color accuracy before applying it to a floorcloth.

3. Wear latex gloves when sponging. Some acrylic paints contain stains that are difficult to remove from the skin. Drop a natural sea sponge into a bucket of water and wring out the excess. Dip the sponge into the sponging medium and squeeze it out gently, leaving the sponge fairly well loaded with paint.

Dabbing a sponge over canvas

4. Dab the sponge unevenly over the desired surface of the canvas. Reload the sponge with sponging medium as it begins to lose its stamping quality. It takes a little practice to produce an even texture; keeping the same amount of paint in your sponge will help. Turn the sponge regularly and twist your wrist to change the direction of the sponge pattern. Allow the medium to dry thoroughly.

A wide variety of sponges are available at craft, art supply, bath, and paint stores and can be used to create a range of painted effects. Generally, natural sponges produce the most natural texture. They have an uneven structure, so different parts of the sponge produce different patterns. One part of the sponge might be finely grained, while other areas may have large open holes that will give you a coarse texture.

Cellulose sponges, like the ones people use for washing their dishes, have more consistently sized holes and a straight edge. They produce a less interesting effect but can be incorporated into a design. Think about cutting sponges into stars, squares, or other simple shapes to make an interesting pattern.

Start collecting different types and shapes of sponges. Experiment with them to see the variety of textures you can achieve. One will be just right for your next project.

Ragging

The opposite of sponging, ragging is a "negative" application. After applying paint to an existing base coat, you remove random areas of wet paint with paper towels and cotton rags to expose the layer beneath. Ragging medium and sponging medium are prepared using the same proportions of water, extender, and acrylic paint. Ragging works with either light-on-dark or dark-on-light applications. Experiment with the technique to see what works best for you.

MATERIALS

- Canvas floorcloth prepared with base coat
- Acrylic paint
- Wide-mouth plastic container
- 1 tbsp. (15 ml) paint extender
- ⅛ cup (30 ml) water
- Scrap canvas
- Latex gloves
- 2-in. (5 cm) housepainter's brush
- Paper towels
- Cloth rags (optional)

1. Prepare the canvas floorcloth and apply a base coat. Allow the paint to dry thoroughly.

2. Squeeze a quarter-size blob of acrylic paint into a wide-mouth plastic container and add 1 tablespoon (15 ml) of paint extender. The extender allows the acrylic to flow smoothly when mixed with water. It also extends the drying time, which allows you to work with the entire surface to even out all areas. Add ⅛ cup (30 ml) of water and stir thoroughly to create a smooth liquid. Always test a small sample on scrap canvas and allow it to dry to check for color accuracy before applying it to a floorcloth.

3. Since this is another hands-on painting method, wear latex gloves. Using a 2-inch (5 cm) house painter's brush, apply the ragging medium over the dry base coat. Crumple up a piece of paper towel and randomly dab off the wet paint. Different types of paper towels leave different patterns. Try several brands to find the pattern that is most pleasing to your eye.

Practice ragging on a scrap of canvas to get the effect you want. Start with a dark color over a lighter one to see the variety of patterns you can create with different ragging techniques.

4. If you use a cloth rag bunched into a wrinkled ball, you can randomly apply or remove the ragging medium. Generally, the cotton-rag method works best for larger areas of color. The differences between ragging on and ragging off are subtle. Explore the possibilities.

Removing and applying paint with a rag

FIXING GOOF-UPS

The techniques described in this chapter can be a little tricky. The best way to avoid mistakes is to practice on scrap canvas until you are sure you've mastered the effect you want. Also, make enough wash or medium to cover all the parts of your floorcloth that you intend to wash or sponge. Even with very careful measuring, it is difficult to replicate colors exactly. If you are not happy with a certain effect, paint over it with another base coat. Notice, though, that every coat of paint erases the natural weave of the canvas somewhat.

Marbling

MATERIALS

- 3 or 4 canvas scraps prepared with base coat in color #1
- Iron
- Acrylic paint, colors #2 and #3
- 2 glass or plastic containers
- 1 tbsp. (15 ml) paint conditioner
- ¼ cup (60 ml) water
- House painter's brush
- Wide-mouth plastic container
- 1 tbsp. (15 ml) paint extender
- ⅛ cup (30 ml) water
- 2-in. (5 cm) house painter's brush
- #6 liner brush
- Damp sponge
- #6 fan brush or 1-in. (2.5 cm) flat bristle brush
- Photograph or real piece of marble

Marble has been used as a floor treatment for centuries. It seems only natural to apply "faux" marble techniques to an entryway floorcloth or a grand dining room rug. Painters have been mimicking marble for as long as it has been around, and there are several wonderful books that go into great detail about the most realistic ways to reproduce every type of existing stone. If the effect appeals to you, by all means search out those instructions.

Here I present a basic approach to the topic. With a few brush strokes and some liberties, the following steps show how to make canvas look like marble. When used in combination with other textural techniques, marbling unveils designs with depth and a certain classic charm.

COLOR CHOICES

Use these same colors or select your own combination using the color code below. Names of paint colors vary from brand to brand, so I won't use specific color names. Simply take this book to the paint store and match the swatches.

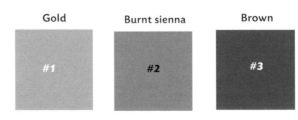

Gold	Burnt sienna	Brown
#1	#2	#3

1. For a first practice attempt, start with a light base coat. It is more forgiving and will give you an immediate sense of accomplishment. Prepare three or four scraps of canvas with a base coat in color #1. Allow them to dry and press them (from the back, unpainted side) for a nice, flat surface.

2. Squeeze a dime-size blob of color #2 acrylic paint into a small glass or plastic container. Add 1 tablespoon (15 ml) of paint conditioner and ¼ cup (60 ml) of water and stir thoroughly (this is the same proportion as that used in a wash). Most extenders are cloudy when they are wet and will make the wash look lighter than it will be when it is dry. Always test a small sample on scrap canvas (paper and wood react differently) and let it dry to check for color accuracy before you apply the wash to a floorcloth. In another container, mix equal parts conditioner and water and use a house painter's brush to wet the canvas with the mixture.

3. In a wide-mouth container, prepare a veining medium by combining color #3, paint extender, and water (this is the same proportion as that used in a sponging medium).

4. With a 2-inch (5 cm) house painter's brush, apply a few broad strokes of the wash over the base coat. Even out the wash slightly (a).

5. With a #6 liner brush, loosely scribble the veining medium onto the darkest areas of the wash (b). Veins of marble look most realistic when they are drawn across the diagonal and connected in a few places, like roads on a map. The veins should be continuous and travel off the edge of the painted space.

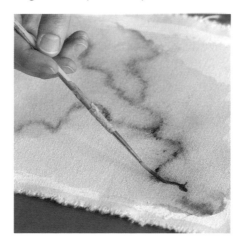

6. With a damp sponge, gently dab the veins to remove any excess paint. Use a #6 fan brush or a flat bristle brush to softly blend the veins into the surrounding wash (c). Don't overwork the painting. The more you practice this skill, the more natural your strokes will become. If the veins begin to wash away, reapply them and resist the temptation to blend too much. Allow the paint to dry completely.

7. When the marbling is dry, put your scrap of canvas on the floor and step back from it. Compare your "marble" with a photograph or a real piece of marble. Decide whether you need to add more veins or wash white over areas that seem too strong. When you are happy with your marbling technique, you are ready to use it on a floorcloth.

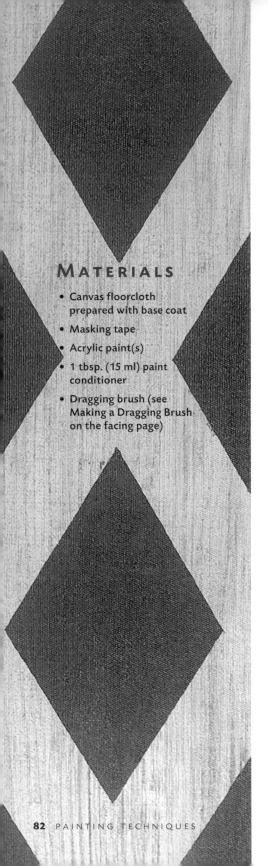

Dragging

Dragging is the process of pulling paint across a canvas surface to create a streaked appearance. Usually this is done on a straight path so that the paint creates a sense of directional movement. Dragging can be done with soft, pastel colors over a white base to create a very subtle texture, or with bold colors over a softer base color, to create a vibrant grain that resembles that of coarse wood.

As with the other painting techniques, experimentation is the most interesting part of the process. Try various colors, paint densities, and types of brushes to see what you can create.

MATERIALS

- Canvas floorcloth prepared with base coat
- Masking tape
- Acrylic paint(s)
- 1 tbsp. (15 ml) paint conditioner
- Dragging brush (see Making a Dragging Brush on the facing page)

1. Prepare a piece of canvas with the base coat and let it dry completely.
2. When applying a dragging effect to specific areas of a floorcloth, you need to tape the surrounding space. This lets you start the drag outside of the intended area and be in mid-drag as you cover the area. The brush usually leaves a heavier amount of paint where it is first put down and where it is lifted off the canvas. If you don't tape off the area, you'll create a very uneven texture.

3. Generally, to produce a successful result, the dragging medium needs to be thick enough to skip over the canvas and yet thin enough to leave an even application of color. Different acrylic paints have varying amounts of body, so you will have to adjust the dragging medium until it works for you.

Start with a dime-size squirt of acrylic paint and add 1 tablespoon (15 ml) of paint conditioner. Blend the mixture evenly. Test the mixture with the dragging brush on a scrap of the base-coated canvas. If the medium is the right consistency, it should go on in stripes, skipping over the canvas. If it bleeds out of the stripes, it is too thin and you need to add more acrylic paint. If it skips too much and leaves a patchy look, it is too thick and should be thinned with a little water.

4. When you are satisfied with the effects, load the brush with dragging medium. Scrape any excess off on the edge of the container. Pull the brush across the canvas with an even pressure. Lift the brush and reload it for each stroke. The trick with dragging is to leave the base color exposed in random areas. After the area is completed, go back and gently touch up spots that seem too skimpy or too heavy.

5. Applying layers of paint can make the dragging technique even more interesting. Try applying several layers of soft pastel colors over a white base coat to create a dreamy, cloudy effect. Allow the dragging medium to dry between layers, or the colors will mingle and become too muddy.

6. Try dragging paint in different directions on subsequent layers to produce interesting patterns. This can be done using the same color to create a woven texture or with different colors to create a more random effect. When dry, the final dragging can be softened with an all-over wash in a related color.

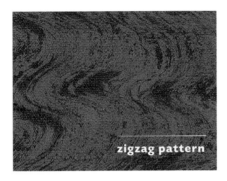

zigzag pattern

wood grain pattern

cross-hatch pattern

MAKING A DRAGGING BRUSH

Buy the cheapest, toughest bristle brushes you can find. Flat 2-inch (5 cm) brushes are the most versatile, but try a variety of sizes for experimentation. With a pair of sharp craft scissors, snip into the bristles vertically to thin the brush. Snip larger chunks here and there, leaving several clumps of bristles at their original length. These will be the bristles that apply the paint.

Wet the brush and squeeze out excess water on a paper towel. Brush water on the paper towel and lift the brush to see whether well-defined clumps of bristles are evident. If not, continue clipping. Try the brush with dragging medium and continue snipping until it applies paint in defined streaks.

FAUX FINISHES

The ancient Egyptians and Chinese used painting techniques to imitate marble and other semiprecious stones. These faux finishes migrated west in the sixteenth century, when Europeans began using the techniques in their architecture. The French claimed that natural stone from Venice had become too expensive and that they were therefore forced to find an alternative way to represent stone in their buildings, hence the adoption of "faux marbling" or "fantasy" finishes.

The Italians, however, claim that it was necessary for them to use inferior building materials because of poor financial conditions in the eighteenth century, so they developed painting techniques to recreate the effect of stone. Regardless of who first adopted these techniques in the West, fantasy finishes became popular throughout Europe and were extremely elaborate and often more detailed and ostentatious than the stone itself.

Distressing

Sanding the base coats of a floorcloth gives the design a casual, somewhat worn appearance that can be very effective with certain styles. Known as distressing, this technique also works nicely if you have applied paint with too heavy a hand. In that case, fine sanding removes the thick build-up of paint without affecting the overall look. To expose the ochre gold paint underneath the rust topcoat on the floorcloth above, the artist sanded the piece in horizontal strips, giving it the effect of naturally worn wood.

Combining Techniques

You can combine washes, sponging, marbling, and dragging to create textures with even more depth and interest. The weave of the canvas provides a base, allowing these techniques to blend and work with the grain of the fabric. Apply a wash of color over the base coat to break up the flat background before you sponge over it. Or sponge on two or three complementary colors (allow each color to dry separately) to create a vibrant, impressionistic quality. Here are some other ideas you may want to try.

- Marbling looks most realistic when applied over a base wash of color. Randomly apply the wash. After it dries, look for the natural "veins" created by the flow of the wash. This is where the painting process gets really fun. Let the direction of the paint show you where to take the next step.

- If a texture looks too harsh, let it dry and apply a wash over that area to soften the effect. Keep in mind that a wash in a complementary color will create a duller, muddier tone. Keep the layers of colors within or near the same color tone to avoid murkiness.

- When creating a floorcloth with a geometric pattern, try using different textural effects on alternating areas. For example, on a checkerboard design, apply a dark shade of sponging on the darker checks and marble the lighter ones for a dramatic design.

- Introduce some direction and movement with the dragging technique to create a subtle backdrop for a more significant foreground detail or a geometric motif.

- Think of textural effects as a way to lead the eye into and around a design. Dark, sponged areas add depth and recede into the background, while light, flat areas appear to come forward. These textural effects do amazing things to change the way we perceive a two-dimensional image.

- Unusual objects can be used to add texture and pattern. Leaves, vegetables, flowers, and feathers can be coated with paint and pressed onto canvas. To create a "negative" of the object, tape it onto the canvas and paint over it.

This floorcloth combines marbled gold squares, ragged red squares, and a gold and red border stamped with a Greek key motif.

Marbled Checks

6 feet x 8 feet (180 cm x 240 cm)

Most marbled floors have a checkerboard pattern, and this design is also the most successful way to reproduce marble on a floorcloth to evoke a classic sense of formality. Making a marbled checkerboard allows you to work in smaller squares, as opposed to broad areas of canvas, which are difficult to keep consistent. Experiment with a variety of marble colors to contrast with the solid colored checks.

MATERIALS

- Prepared canvas, 6 ft. x 8 ft.
- 1 qt. (1 liter) *each* flat finish latex paint, colors #1, #2, and #5
- Small decorator's paintbrush
- 4-in. (10 cm) house painter's brush
- Metal ruler
- Pencil
- Marbled Checks template
- 2 small plastic containers
- 2 oz. (60 ml) *each* tube acrylic paint, colors #3, #4, and #6
- Paint conditioner
- Water
- ½-in. (1 cm) flat brush
- #6 liner brush
- 2-in. (5 cm) flat bristle brush
- ½-in. (1 cm) masking tape
- Craft knife
- Metal spoon
- Wide, shallow, plastic container
- Natural sponge
- Diamond Border template
- Prepared diamond stamp
- Sponge brush
- 1 qt. (1 liter) polyurethane, semigloss finish
- 1 qt. (1 liter) polyurethane, satin finish

COLOR CHOICES

Use these colors or select your own combination using the code below. Names of colors vary from brand to brand, so I won't use specific names. Simply take this book to the paint store and match the swatches.

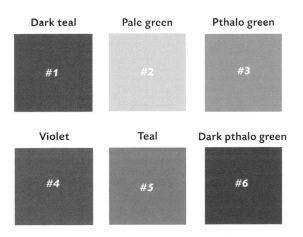

Dark teal	Pale green	Pthalo green
#1	#2	#3

Violet	Teal	Dark pthalo green
#4	#5	#6

Prepare the Floorcloth

1. Paint the back hem of the floor-cloth color #1 with a small decorator's paintbrush. Allow it to dry thoroughly..

2. Turn the floorcloth over and paint the front color #2, using the house painter's brush. Allow it to dry thoroughly.

3. Using the metal ruler, mark 6 inches (15 cm) in from the edge and draw a light pencil line parallel to the edge to form the border. Using the template at right, make marks around the border to act as end-points (see page 133 for a larger template you can photocopy). Connect these marks with light pencil lines to form the checker-boards. In pencil, mark the checks that will be painted color #5.

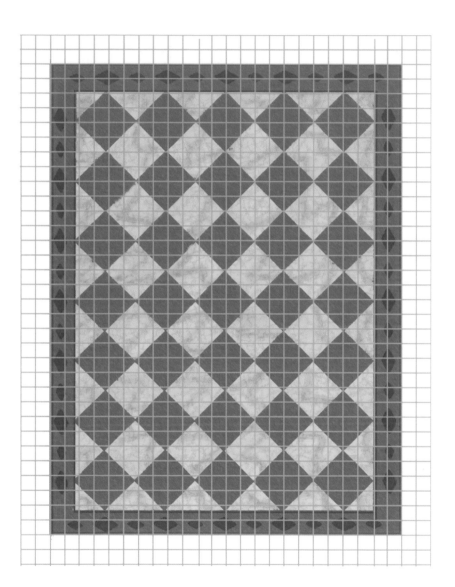

Marbled Checks Template
1 square = 3" (7.5cm)

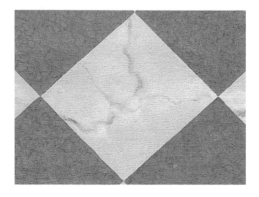

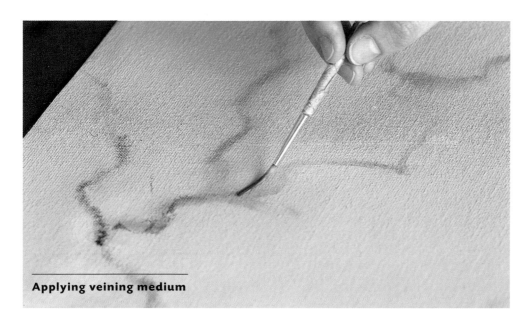

Applying veining medium

Paint the Marbled Checks

1. Prepare the wash medium for marbleizing. In a small plastic container, thin a dime-size blob of color #3 with 1 teaspoon (5 ml) of paint conditioner and 2 teaspoons (10 ml) of water. Then prepare the veining medium in another plastic container using a dime-size blob of color #4, 1 teaspoon (5 ml) of paint conditioner, and 1 teaspoon (5 ml) of water. Mix both solutions well.

2. With the small decorator's brush, paint some water onto one of the squares to be marbleized. Using the ½-inch (1 cm) flat brush, apply the prepared wash medium. Now squiggle on the vein medium with the #6 liner brush. While the paint is still wet, drag the 2-inch flat bristle brush lightly across the surface to blend the veins slightly. Continue the marbling process for all of the marbled squares. Allow the floorcloth to dry overnight.

MAKING THOSE CHECKS FIT

When making different sizes of checked floorcloths, be aware of certain design considerations. As a general rule, the border should be half as wide as the checks. The checks should become larger as the floorcloth grows larger. Too many checks on a large floorcloth will look too busy; too few on a small floor-cloth won't establish the pattern.

Always lay out the pattern on graph paper first. It is easiest to divide the area inside the border into four columns across the short side (or six columns, for larger pieces) and then add rows until you reach the desired length. You can also elongate the checks to obtain the desired length. Add the border last, to see what size looks best. Once it's all worked out on graph paper, you are ready to transfer the pattern to the prepared canvas and paint the floorcloth.

Paint the Sponged Checks

1. Apply masking tape along the border and to the outer edges of the checks that will be painted color #5. Use a craft knife and a metal ruler to cut the corners square. Press the edges of the tape into the canvas using the back of a spoon.

2. Paint all of these squares using the small decorator's brush.

3. Prepare the sponging medium. In a wide, shallow, plastic container, mix 1 tablespoon (15 ml) of color #6 with 1 tablespoon (15 ml) of paint conditioner and enough water to make a milky consistency.

4. Wet the sponge and wring out any excess water. Dab the sponge into the sponging medium and apply it to the checks and the border, varying your hand position to create a random effect. Allow the paint to dry overnight.

5. Using the template at right, prepare the Diamond Stamp. Draw a line on the floorcloth with watercolor pencil to indicate the center of the border. This is where you will stamp the diamond shape

Sponging paint over base coat

around the perimeter. Using a sponge brush, apply color #1 to the stamp and carefully align the stamp before pressing the paint onto the border. Continue applying evenly spaced diamonds to complete the border.

Finish the Floorcloth

1. Carefully remove the masking tape. Using the template on page 88, draw pencil lines where you want the borders to be. Use masking tape if you want very straight lines or paint freehand using the ½-inch flat brush and apply latex paint in color #1. Allow the border to dry thoroughly (about 8 hours).

2. With the house painter's brush, apply 3 coats of semigloss polyurethane for normal traffic, or apply 4 coats for rougher use. Allow at least 8 hours of drying time in between each coat of polyurethane.

3. Apply a final coat of satin polyurethane using the house painter's brush. Allow the floorcloth to cure for at least a week before putting it on the floor.

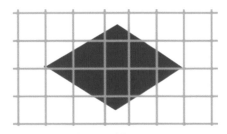

Diamond Stamp
1 square = 1" (2.5 cm)

VARIATIONS ON A THEME

In these three examples of alternative designs, the colors and decorative elements change to suit three very different situations. Keep in mind that the two basic colors should coordinate with each other and relate to key elements within the room. Look at entryways in historic buildings for more color ideas using the checkerboard pattern.

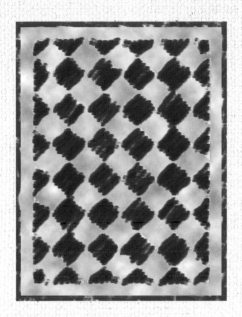

Sky Blue and Lilac Checks
6 feet x 6 feet (180 cm x 180 cm)

The soft blue squares create a dreamy, cloudlike effect, while the dark lilac squares set off the pattern. The dark lilac is striped around the outside border to create a visual stop for the sky, which needs to be contained or the peaceful space may wander right off the edge of the floorcloth.

To make this design, apply a base coat of white on the entire floorcloth, then wash sky blue over it. Pencil the checks and border over the background, then paint the lilac squares with loose, free strokes; work in a slightly darker lilac paint while the first coat is still wet. Seal the floorcloth with polyurethane.

Blue and Gold Checks with Sunflowers
2½ feet x 3¾ feet (75 cm x 112.5 cm)

This countrylike pattern has vivid hand-painted sunflowers and leaves, which add rhythm to an already strong background of summery blue and gold.

To make this design, paint the entire floorcloth blue. Pencil the checks and border over the background. Paint the squares gold, then apply an orange wash. Next, paint the green border and large green leaves. Finally, paint large, loose sunflowers in several colors of orange, yellow, and gold, and then add brown centers. Seal the floorcloth with polyurethane.

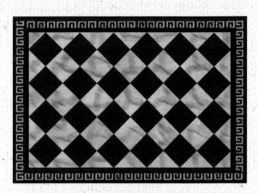

Greek Key Bordered Checks
6 feet x 9 feet (180 cm x 270 cm)

The sponging technique is used on the deep red areas, which alternate with marbled gold. For added interest, the Greek key pattern creates a beautiful border.

To make this design, paint the entire floorcloth pale gold, then apply a slightly darker gold wash. Paint the marbling in burnt sienna and iridescent gold. Pencil the diamonds and border over the background. Tape off the areas that will be painted red. Paint the alternating diamonds red. Use the sponging technique (see page 76) to apply a darker red color. When the paint is dry, remove the tape. Make a stamp (see page 42) of the Greek key motif and stamp the pattern around the border using the gold base coat. When the stamped pattern is dry, wash over the key motif with iridescent gold. For added drama, paint border stripes in black. Seal the floorcloth with polyurethane.

Wreaths and Squares, 6 feet x 8 feet

A Gallery of Floorcloths

NOW THAT YOU'VE LEARNED THE BASIC SKILLS involved in making a floorcloth, you're ready to create some of your own designs. This gallery section is here specifically for that purpose. Each of the artists represented started creating his or her unique designs at some point in time. With patience, practice, and courage they have ventured into this wonderful world of floorcloth painting and are creating beautiful pieces for homes far and wide.

I operate my business, Canvasworks, in a quaint, historic town in Vermont. My studio and showroom are in the carriage house wing of a 200-year-old house where old beams, wide-board floors, and views of age-old maples and stone walls prevail. This has led me down a creative path of historical colors and geometric designs that were popular hundreds of years ago. Most of my floorcloths are large, custom-made pieces for colonial-, country-, and early American-style homes. Each piece decorates my studio while I'm working on it. More often than not, I'm sad to see them go when the delivery truck comes to ship them away. *Photograph by Lisa Curry Mair.*

Orbo Design

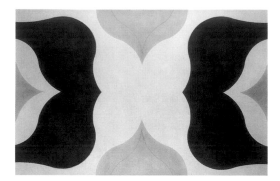

Curves, 6 feet x 9 feet

Painter Kristin Ordahl and furniture designer Kelly Bortoluzzi combined their talents and the first syllables of their last names to create Orbo Design, which produces hand-painted canvas rugs. They launched their business in Williamsburg, Brooklyn, in December 1999. Their goal is to make canvas rugs with modern materials, thereby reinventing the tradition of the floorcloth. The rugs are decidedly contemporary, reflecting new techniques of painting with acrylic stains and polymer sealants. Influences include the Minimalist paintings of Agnes Martin; the stripes on vintage ticking; Far Eastern rugs; the Arts and Crafts movement; and Near Eastern, Indian, and modernist textiles, such as those of Alexander Girard and Marimekko.

This fresh approach has brought the designers to the attention of such tastemakers as Martha Stewart, who was so pleased with the custom rugs that Orbo Design made for her potting shed that she invited Kristin and Kelly to appear on her television show in February 2001. Numerous architects, among them Robert A.M. Stern, whose firm commissioned several custom rugs for a client in Nantucket, Massachusetts, have also come calling. *Photographs by Beth Schneckenburger.*

Bands, 2½ feet x 9 feet

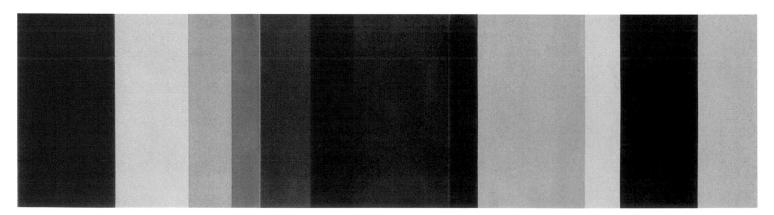

Colavita 32, 32 inches x 32 inches

"To create a unified palette, we start with a field of color and then apply transparent stains on top. We often use contrasting colors to set off shapes, such as the hot red and cool yellow detail lines in this piece."

Susan Arnold

Fish, 3 feet x 4 feet

These two floorcloths were made with hand-cut stencils and small, hand-cut stamps.

Susan Arnold lives in Vermont with her husband and four children. Through her hobby of applying decorative painting to walls, cabinets, and floors, she developed techniques that she then used to make floorcloths.

As an artist, Susan is inspired by creating new patterns and color variations. She particularly enjoys fashioning her canvases after Oriental carpets and kilims. Her business, Folk Floors Studio, produces hand-painted rugs, table runners, placemats, tablecloths, and pet food mats. *Photographs by G. B. Hubbard.*

Coffee Cups, 3 feet x 4 feet

Leaves, 5 feet x 7 feet

The leaves on this piece were created by cutting out porous packing material to achieve a textured stamping surface.

Sandy Ducharme

Sandy Ducharme has always enjoyed art and developed a love of watercolor painting prior to exploring acrylics and floorcloths. Her floorcloth studio is located at the nursery she owns and operates. Sandy is a juried member of the Vermont Handcrafters, the Vermont Craft Council, and the Vermont Craft Producers. She displays her work at craft shows throughout Vermont and neighboring New England states and received the Best of Show award for the Hildene Arts Festival 2000. Several Vermont handcraft specialty stores carry her floorcloths, pet mats, placemats, and table runners.

Sandy writes, "In finishing a free-hand floorcloth, I often wait to do the border until the rest of the piece is done. I draw inspiration from the design and colors to tie in the border and complement the piece. This allows more freedom with the overall style. I love creating free-hand designs and use my gardens as inspiration. I'm also a true nature lover and use Mother Nature as a source of inspiration — sunsets, birds, butterflies, wildflowers, the ocean, and the way the trees move in the wind." *Photograph by Alan Hebert.*

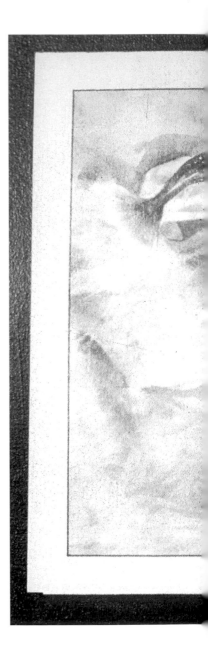

Goldfish, 2 feet x 3 feet

The background pool effect on this piece was made by layering several shades of blue and neutral tones to achieve a dappled appearance. The goldfish were painted last and seem to be looking into the pool, casting their shadows into the watery depths.

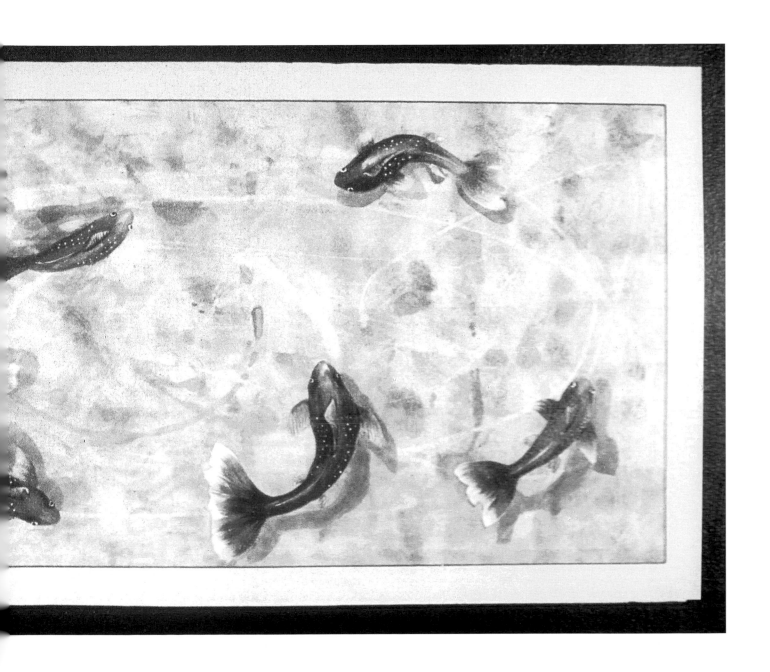

Linda Arthurs

Linda Arthurs attended the Ontario College of Art, is a member of the Ontario Craft Council, and has paintings in permanent collections in London and Amsterdam. She is a retired art director. Linda shows her work at various craft shows and her business, Art on the Floor, does custom work for decorators.

Linda fell in love with floorcloths while having coffee with a friend who had one on her kitchen floor. She notes, "I use absolutely everything to make floorcloths, including linoleum, heavy canvas, oil and acrylic paints, paper, wallpaper books, and fabric swatches. I love to experiment with new materials." Linda finds inspiration (as well as fabrics) during her many travels and is motivated by bright colors and the idea of bringing beauty into other people's homes. *Photographs by Linda Arthurs.*

Leaves on Black,

2⅓ feet x 8 feet

This piece was made with sponged, scrapped, stenciled, and hand-painted techniques.

Fern Runner and detail,

2⅓ feet x 12 feet

This floorcloth was created with fresh ferns, which were coated with paint and pressed onto the primed surface to create a print. It was a messy process, but the natural appearance of the finished piece made the effort well worth it.

Natalie Browne-Gutnik

A lifelong handcrafter, Natalie Browne-Gutnik took a floorcloth class at age 49 and became hooked on the craft. She went home and told her husband she wanted to be a floorcloth artist and do major outdoor art fairs when she grew up. That was in 1992. Today, her company, Natasha Floor and Wall Cloths, specializes in custom-designed, one-of-a-kind painted canvases. Her husband, Marty, does the preliminary canvas preparation and show setups and takedowns, which allows Natalie the time to design and paint.

Natalie writes, "Floorcloths have the unique advantage of being situated in areas where they are seen from multiple locations. Consequently, a floorcloth can become a unifier of diverse colors and motifs. For instance, the most popular places for floorcloths are in front of the kitchen sink, in an entryway, or under a kitchen or dining room table. These are all areas from which other rooms extend. By using the floorcloth as a unifier, a cohesive decorating scheme can be achieved."

Natalie's floorcloths are created to be used as floor or wall coverings and are painted in the round, ensuring that they have a unique composition when viewed from each of the four sides. She also uses silk screening, masking, marbling, sponging, stenciling, spattering, and ragging techniques. Most of her designs consist of geometric, abstract, and organic forms that create a sense of fun. Natalie uses a vivid color palette of primary hues to create a narrative that reflects her world view of the abundance of life on Earth and the interdependency of all its living creatures. *Photographs by F. Fischer.*

African Contemporary,
6½ feet x 3 feet

Coral Reef, 5½ feet x 4 feet

"When I paint a floorcloth, I make sure that each side of the canvas has its own composition. In this piece, sea creatures are swimming around the leaves and smiling face of an underwater tree. Turning the floorcloth 90 degrees to the left, the image changes to a red brick path in an enchanted land."

Skip Dyrda

Rainy Day Play, 2½ feet x 4 feet

The artist painted the coloring book and other props from real items but drew the old linoleum from his imagination.

Skip Dyrda owns and operates New World Productions, the gallery and studio where he creates commissioned floorcloths, murals, fine art, and occasionally sculpture. He specializes in using the trompe l'oeil style, especially for his floorcloths. His projects include a large, five-story mural that was voted one of the best examples of public art in Sarasota, Florida.

"Several years ago I shared studio space with a decorative artist. It was then that I started doing Trompe L'oeil, without even knowing I was doing it. I was always interested in details and painting the illusion of objects on a rug grew from there. For my commissioned floorcloths, I have to figure out what my clients want. But usually, that part is only the background. Then I have fun with painting objects that have some kind of connection to the client. Many times I have trouble getting visitors to enter my gallery simply because they don't want to step on the artwork." *Photographs by Skip Dyrda, except for that of* Rainy Day Play, *which is by Tom Jeffords.*

Adventures in Patioland I,
40 inches x 60 inches

This floorcloth depicts the daily routine of the creatures one might find crawling around the average Florida patio — a frog, a lizard, a large spider, and an army of ants, among others.

Where's Fido?, 6½ feet x 24 feet

Parts of this floorcloth were painted with an airbrush. Lying about are signs that
Fido was indeed in the area — his black leash, a chewed-up rubber ball, and a note
from the artist and the artist's brush. Fido no doubt scared the artist off.

Karen Calabrese

Old Wood Flag,

22 inches x 32 inches

"An old wooden doormat inspired me to paint this floorcloth with cracked wooden slats and worn, peeling paint. Using very heavy canvas allows me to cut the edges with indentations that resemble real wood, which brings more realism to the piece."

Leopard Skin,

20 inches x 28 inches

"My projects begin with an idea and evolve as I paint. This floorcloth began with the leopard's face. As I applied fur to the head, I decided not to paint the body but to create undulating areas that make the body seem to emerge from the background."

Although she has always been creative, Karen Calabrese once put her dreams aside to concentrate on raising a family. In 1991, she turned back to her art, beginning with pencil portraits and pen and ink drawings. Her artistic interests are diverse, and a natural progression led her to paint on canvas. Mounted canvas felt too confining, and this led her to create murals, canvas wall art, and floorcloths.

Karen says, "A lot of research and experimentation finally allowed me to produce hemless, freeform floorcloths that lie flat on the floor without buckling. I have always loved the look of old floorcloths, but my interests lean more toward trompe l'oeil than pure design. I love to create something unusual — something to make people smile — that is unrestricted by a rectangular border. I am especially happy if someone reaches down to touch something on my floorcloth, just to see if it's really what it appears to be." *Photographs by Karen Calabrese.*

The Monarch, 17 inches x 22 inches

"I'm fascinated with butterflies and the translucent quality of their wings. For this floorcloth, I began with an undercoat of bright yellow paint followed by several washes of burnt sienna. The undercoat glows through the top layers, creating the transparency I needed.

To create a floorcloth with an interesting shape, I use very heavy #6 canvas, and paint and seal both sides. This creates a very heavy floorcloth that is flexible and lies flat without a hem. I cut out the shape just before applying the final coats of sealer."

Arlene Crooks-Best

Arlene Crooks-Best started making floorcloths at the request of a friend. "My friend saw one in a decorating book that I had and asked me if I could make one for her. That was the first one I did and I haven't stopped making them yet. I love them, because the sky is the limit." In 1988 Arlene established Ar Works, a small, in-home business that specializes in custom-made floorcloths, canvases, and faux-finished furniture. Her clients include Balzac's Coffee Roastery, Anything Grows, The Dressing Room, Victoria Costumière, the Arden Restaurant, and the Stratford Festival Theatre Store, all based in Stratford, Ontario. Her work can be seen in homes across Canada, the United States, and Jamaica.

Arlene has been active as a designer and artist for The Stratford Designer Showcase Home, and her floorcloths have been sold at the I Love My Gallery Auction to benefit the Gallery Stratford. She has taught floorcloth making for the Gallery Stratford, the Stratford-Perth Museum, and the Handworks Festival held in Kitchener, Ontario. *Photographs by Arlene Crooks-Best.*

Leopard Print, 6 feet x 9 feet

This floorcloth is painted on single piece of linoleum. The artist primed the linoleum, painted base coats, then applied glaze along the borders with a dragging technique. Each leopard spot was painted individually.

Forever Peace, 10 feet x 12 feet

This floorcloth was designed as a life-size board game for a Mennonite Peace Conference. Children acted as chess pieces and moved around the board.

Lori Fusello

At a young age Lori Fusello developed an interest in historical architecture and decorative design from the turn of the 20th century, La Belle Époque. She came to feel great kinship and inspiration from the artists and designers who flourished during the Arts and Crafts period, the English Aesthetic Movement, the Art Nouveau period, and the poster art movement. Like those artists, Lori believes we have an inherent need to surround ourselves in daily life with functional, beautiful art executed with skilled craftsmanship.

Lori opened La Belle Époque Studios in 1998. Her floorcloths, wallcloths, and other home textiles combine the two great passions in her life: the need to create beautiful things with her own hands and her love of period-inspired decorative arts. She notes, "What better way to pay homage to the artists, craftsmen, and philosophies I admire so much than to keep their art and ideas alive through my own?" *Photographs by Jerry McCollum.*

Abstract Able,

2 feet x 3 feet

Created as an accent piece for a neutral-colored room, this floorcloth was painted with layers of stippled washes to create richer colors and a greater sense of depth.

JOB, 41 inches x 55 inches

Inspired by Alphonse Mucha's art poster for JOB cigarette papers, this floorcloth was built up layer by translucent layer, with a swirled watercolor effect for the hair. It was made for clients with the last name of Job and is definitely the center of attention in their living room!

Harlequin Shuffle, 35 inches x 42 inches

This floorcloth was inspired by an ancient Greek amphora vessel. The background was painted in mottled washes of ochre, sienna, and umber. The harlequin design and "shuffling" animals add just the right touch of whimsy.

Debra Gould

Pre-Columbian Twins, 37 inches x 51 inches

Both floorcloths were painted in brown, gold, and ochre glazes, which were applied in layers using sponges and rags. The designs were drawn freehand, and masking tape was used to provide a clean edge when necessary.

Debra Gould studied art in Montreal and silversmithing in Mexico and Toronto. But this training was not the focus of her first career. An MBA graduate with a successful Toronto-based career consulting to Fortune 500 companies, Debra decided at age 40 that it was time to try something new. She always wondered what would have happened if she had used her early art training rather than following a more secure profession. Closing her consulting company and selling or giving away most of her belongings, Debra moved to the remote island of Salt Spring, British Columbia, in 1998. In the quiet of the countryside, she began her internal search for how she might follow her heart in the second half of her life.

After some experimentation, Debra found she loved the idea of art you can walk on and felt that the surprising durability and practicality of floorcloths made them so appropriate for today's hectic lifestyle. She now works full-time designing, painting, and marketing her creations from her studio in Victoria, British Columbia. Thanks to the Internet, clients in Canada, the United States, and Australia collect her floorcloths, table art, mirrors, boxes, trays, clocks, shower curtains, and pillows.

Debra is committed to functional art as a focus for her business. "We're surrounded by functional objects, usually mass produced and not necessarily that fun or interesting to look at," she says. "By introducing a few handcrafted items into our homes we create a unique environment and bring our rooms to life." A passion for color is evident in Debra's Home Collection. Her designs are loosely grouped into six theme areas: Asian, Sophisticates, Naturals, Primitives, Whimsical, and Wild Things. All her items are hand-painted, signed originals, with no two exactly alike. *Photographs by Debra Gould.*

Joyful, 36 inches x 33 inches

Janet Harris

When Janet Harris and her husband purchased an 1885 brownstone in Brooklyn, New York, in 1990, Janet started pondering how to paint the parlor floor. After reading books about paint finishes, she ragged and marbleized the walls of the entire parlor, with its 14-foot-high ceilings, and was forever hooked on paint finishes. She then became intrigued by the basic techniques for painting floorcloths.

Janet remarks, "I painted my first floorcloth to use under my dining room table. It served a dual purpose at that time. First, it was completely impervious to any food or drink my then one-year-old son might throw on it from his high chair, and second, as floorcloths were widely used in the nineteenth century, it seemed right for the house. Over the years I have painted more than twenty floorcloths for the various houses we have lived in since then." *Photographs by Giles Prett.*

Tile Kitchen Runners,

32 inches x 80 inches

These runners were inspired by a tile pattern and were made to coordinate with the green slate countertops in the artist's kitchen.

Rust and Gold, 35 inches x 35 inches

The artist painted the entire square metallic gold, overpainted it in rust with loose brush strokes, then taped off sections and stenciled the leaves.

Burnt Orange Hallway Runner, 30 inches x 172 inches

To create this piece, the artist painted the entire surface an ochre gold, then overpainted it a rich orange hue. When the top coat was dry, she sanded it until she could see the ochre underneath.

Mary Lou Keith

Swedish Traditional,
26 inches x 36 inches

The words on this floorcloth translate as "Better a little dirt in the corner than a clean Hell."

Mary Lou Keith's interest in floorcloths grew out of the small wooden folk art company she started with her husband. She writes, "I was really excited to get involved with an art form that was so representative of the area in which I live. My home was built in 1785 and is near one of the world's most beautiful harbors, so it's fitting for me to pursue this particular art form, which is so steeped in maritime tradition. I began painting traditional patterns (hooked rugs, quilts, and china patterns) and eventually blended into the mix my own original designs. Surrounded as I am by nautical history, inspiration is never a problem. And, as relatives on both sides of my family are Swedish, I take particular pleasure in producing floorcloths with Scandinavian designs." Her business, Studio 14, sells what Mary Lou calls "floorhangings," works of art to hang on your floor. *Photographs by Mary Lou Keith.*

Poppies, 3 feet x 5 feet

"This piece was made with stencils I cut myself, sponging techniques, and freehand painting."

The Village, 3 feet x 5 feet

"The background of this piece is mottled with a sponge and includes six colors. I created stencils to position the houses, then painted the finishing details by hand. The trees were painted freehand with odd little birds scattered in the branches for fun. This piece was a commissioned work with the recipient's Victorian home included in the design."

Douglas Paisley

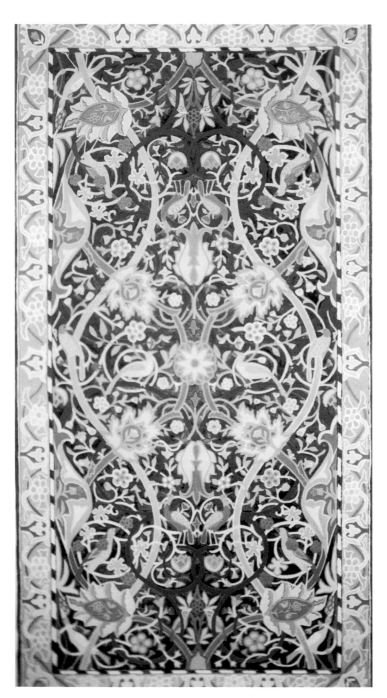

Douglas Paisley paints floorcloths as well as murals and ceilings in clients' homes. He is presently at work on two public murals, one for a bakery in Massachusetts and another for an elementary school in Connecticut. "The floorcloth is important to me," he explains, "because it represents an intense involvement with traditional pattern and decoration (in this case, a close study of William Morris), which is an essential aspect of my more representational and figurative work as a muralist. This floorcloth, like all of my commissioned work, was painted for a specific site, composed and colored-keyed with the surroundings for which it was intended.

I like floorcloths for their practicality (this one has survived several years on a busy restaurant floor with occasional sponge cleanings). But I also love them for their original hand-painted surfaces. The tradition of painting walls, ceilings, floors, and furniture goes back thousands of years before easel painting. It's a pleasure to have as my job this ancient and fundamental task of enlivening rooms where people live with color and invention." *Photographs by Giles Prett.*

William Morris Pattern, 41 inches x 82 inches

To make this floorcloth, the artist first painted the dark blue background using artist's acrylics thinned with matte medium. This allows the weave of the canvas to show through, giving the piece a textured, carpetlike appearance. Then he painted the design one color at a time.

Pam Richt Testerman

Country French, 5 feet x 5 feet

The colors in this floorcloth came from the wallpaper in the client's kitchen. The octagon shape is perfect for the center of the room, where it can be viewed equally well from all angles.

Elephants, 34 inches x 52 inches

The colors for this floorcloth were matched to the client's wallpaper. The room had an exotic feel to it, hence the elephants and the Oasis border design, which was adapted from a commercial stencil that the artist simplified and then handpainted.

Pamela Testerman has studied art her entire life and continues to take art and design courses several times a year. After 15 years in the business of interior drapery design, she started her business, Custom Canvas Design, in 1998. She paints anything on canvas, from floorcloths to murals, from chairs to umbrellas.

"I got into floorcloths because of designers wanting a more professional-grade rug product. I enjoy working with designers and their clients to produce original custom rugs. The colors, patterns, fabrics, and wallpaper clients have chosen for their homes inspire my designs. Floorcloths are an extension of art for the floors. We decorate our walls and sometimes our ceilings but often forget the floor is a wonderful place for original art, as well." *Photographs by Pam Richt Testerman.*

Celtic Design, 4½ feet x 4½ feet

This piece was inspired by Celtic designs, which are created with one continuous line to represent the continuity of the universe. The background is marbled and shadowed to create a three-dimensional effect; the light, natural colors produce the illusion of stone.

Alan Vaughn

Ellis Island One, 4 feet x 6 feet

"This piece was inspired by the hand-cut marble floors at Ellis Island in New York. I painted each tile with a 1-inch brush for an uneven, handmade look."

Alan Vaughn received his formal art training from Virginia Tech, Radford University, and Illinois State University. He taught art at the college level for 11 years and continues teaching in adult programs and community art centers. He began Alan Vaughn Studios in 1987. Since 1991 he has been creating one-of-a-kind and limited edition handcrafted floorcloths as a full-time business. Alan has shown in numerous one-person, invitational, and juried exhibitions.

His work has received many awards and is included in private and corporate collections throughout the United States. He says, "All craftspeople who make truly functional work must serve the dual masters of artistry and practicality. As a maker of floorcloths, I am an art maker and a rug maker. I find this interplay of roles interesting and at the center of my work. However, I am more interested in making a painting for the floor than an object that looks like a rug. It is intriguing to observe individual reactions to stepping on them. Some people will, some won't. But almost everyone seeks permission of some sort. I've come to accept 'Oh, I couldn't' as high praise." *Photographs by Alan Vaughn except for that of* Circular CDR with Spokes, *which is by Sue Ann Kuhn-Smith.*

Shaped CDR, 4 feet x 6 feet

"I enjoy depicting the illusion of depth on a flat surface. This floorcloth plays with the edges of the design to create a three-dimensional look. "

Circular CDR with Spokes, 5½ feet in diameter

"My process for finishing the edges of my rugs requires that the lines be straight to ensure a more durable hem. Look closely and you will see that the outside edge is made of many short straight lines rather than a single curve. This floorcloth, created to go under a round table, is a good example of the great depth and movement that a circular design can offer."

Linda Curran

Linda Curran has been producing floorcloths since 1983. After making a few for her home she realized she had a marketable product and started a business called Country Canvas. Her technique is the result of trial and error, experimentation, and rigorous testing in her home. Linda sells her work through Eastern Ontario craft shows and retailers, and her floorcloths have been shipped all over the world. She produces approximately 200 floorcloths a year, as well as placemats and mousepads. A large portion of her business includes designing custom pieces and teaching floorcloth workshops. Her artistry has been featured in *The Ottawa Citizen* and on local television.

"As an animal lover," she writes, "my inspiration comes from observing animal interactions with each other and with human beings. When I'm painting an animal, it is important to me that there is a sense of communication in the finished work. I find painting floorcloths more satisfying than painting a piece to be framed; it's a challenge to create something meant to be viewed from above. This is a passionate art for me, and I doubt that I will ever retire from it."
Photographs by Wolfgang Grambart.

Content Cat, 36 inches x 48 inches

"To create this floorcloth, I first painted the grout-colored base coat. I drew the cat on clear mac-tac, then cut it out and positioned it on the canvas to protect the area while I painted the mosaic tiles. I cut potatoes in various shapes and sizes to make stamps for the mosaic design. This technique produced the look and feel of worn tiles. After the tiles were done, I removed the mac-tac and painted the cat freehand. A shadow around the cat completes the effect."

Forest Mosaic,
36 inches x 56 inches

"To create this floorcloth I first sketched the pattern on blank canvas, then painted the various grout colors. I stamped the entire piece with potatoes that were cut to fit where needed."

Linda Locke

Sonoran Fiesta, 2½ feet x 6 feet

Full of the desire to express herself artistically but too structured for the free-flow of the traditional artist's canvas, Linda Locke was thunderstruck by her first encounter with the floorcloth. Here was her medium! The design of a floorcloth requires "structured" creativity, and Linda has found that her unique blend of organization and artistry is a perfect combination when it comes to designing floorcloths.

For Linda, the creation of each floorcloth is an adventure. "As the design is planned and the colors are selected, I incorporate my organization and attention to detail acquired from years in the computer industry with my quest for discovery and challenge," she explains. With each new floorcloth she designs, her quest for exploration and experimentation begins anew. *Photograph at left by Linda Locke; photograph below by Dan Delaney.*

Trails Across the Desert,

3 feet x 5 feet

"My goal in creating this piece was to coordinate the floorcloth with the colors and upholstery in the client's living room. It is easier to blend contrasting colors with printed fabric than with paint. The secret is the choice of base color. I used a color called Tucson Clay; when the bolder colors were brushed over it they became more muted. The motifs echo those in the upholstery and are arranged with a border and a center, as in traditional rug design."

Pamela Marwede

Pamela Marwede studied graphic design in Barcelona and calligraphy and fashion and textiles in London. She creates custom floorcloths, murals, hand-painted fabrics, furniture, and glassware for clients through interior design firms in Europe and the United States. Pamela also has a complete line of hand-painted tiles that are available through exclusive tile retailers. Her work has been featured in numerous publications, and she has received the House and Garden "New Designers" Award for her fabrics. Pamela's work is exhibited regularly in art galleries and has been included in a variety of ASID Designer Showcase homes in southwestern Florida. *Photographs by Pamela Marwede.*

Lily Pond, 4 feet x 6 feet

This piece was commissioned to introduce aquatic imagery into a kitchen that was designed using the principles of feng shui. The lilies and vegetation add a sense of serenity and softness. (Collection of Sally Trout.)

Circling Fish, 5½ feet x 5½ feet

This floorcloth was created for the kitchen in a waterfront home. (Entire cloth above, detail below.) The fish are painted with sparkling metallic and interference paints that shimmer and change color when viewed from different angles. Walking over this floorcloth produces the sensation of gliding over a real pool of water. (Collection of Dr. and Mrs. Scheible.)

Patterns

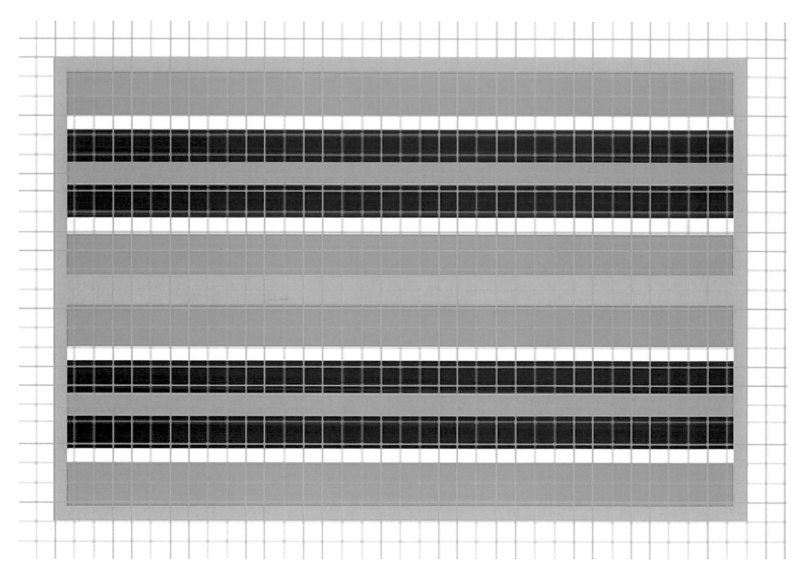

Basic Stripes Template
1 square = 1" (2.5 cm)

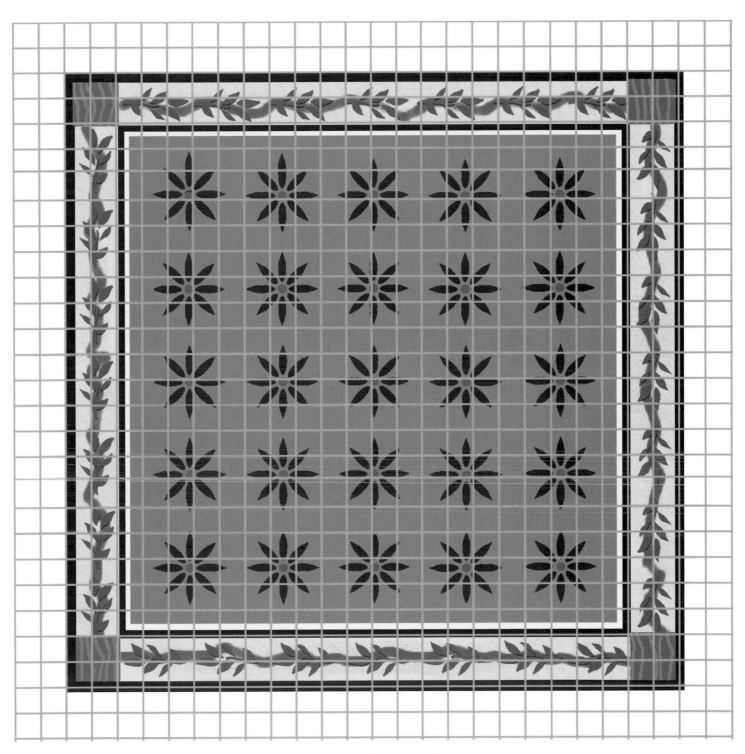

Flowers and Sprigs Template
1 square = 3" (7.5 cm)

Patterns

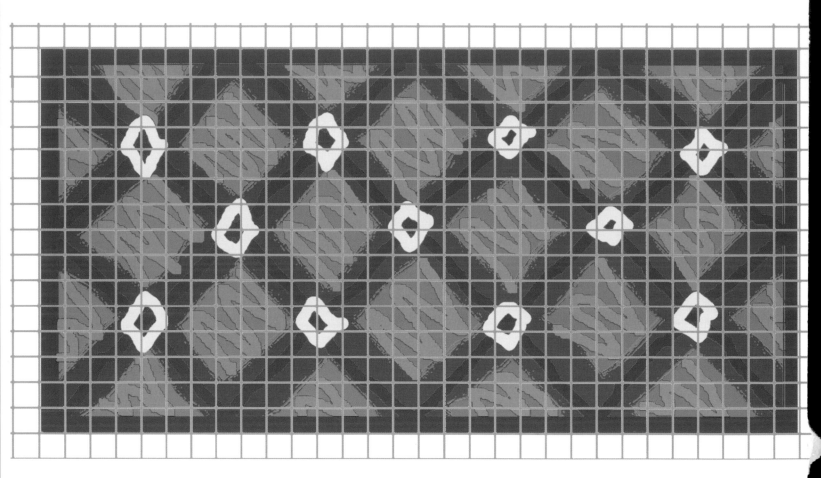

Freehand Plaid Template
1 square = 2" (5 cm)

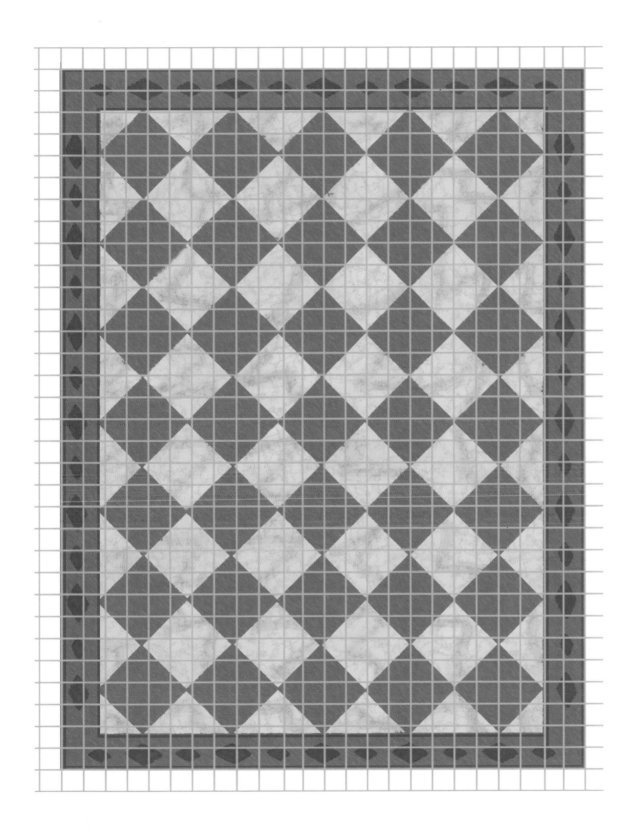

Marbled Checks Template
1 square = 3" (7.5cm)

Metric Conversion Charts

Unless you have finely calibrated measuring equipment, conversions between U.S. and metric measurements will be inexact. It's important to convert all the measurements for a specific project to maintain the proportions used in the original.

GENERAL FORMULAS FOR METRIC CONVERSION

Ounces to grams	multiply ounces by 28.35
Grams to ounces	multiply grams by 0.035
Pounds to grams	multiply pounds by 453.5
Pounds to kilograms	multiply pounds by 0.45
Cups to liters	multiply cups by 0.24
Inches to centimeters	multiply inches by 2.5
Centimeters to inches	multiply centimeters by 0.4
Feet to meters	multiply feet by 0.3
Meters to feet	multiply meters by 3.3

APPROXIMATE METRIC EQUIVALENTS BY WEIGHT

U.S.	METRIC
¼ ounce	7 grams
½ ounce	14 grams
1 ounce	28 grams
1¼ ounces	35 grams
1½ ounces	40 grams
2½ ounces	70 grams
4 ounces	112 grams
5 ounces	140 grams
8 ounces	228 grams
10 ounces	280 grams
15 ounces	425 grams
16 ounces (1 pound)	454 grams

APPROXIMATE METRIC EQUIVALENTS BY VOLUME

U.S.	METRIC
1 teaspoon	5 milliliters
1 tablespoon	15 milliliters
¼ cup	60 milliliters
½ cup	120 milliliters
1 cup	230 milliliters
1¼ cups	300 milliliters
1½ cups	360 milliliters
2 cups	460 milliliters
2½ cups	600 milliliters
3 cups	700 milliliters
4 cups (1 quart)	0.95 liter
1.06 quarts	1 liter
4 quarts (1 gallon)	3.8 liters

Contributing Artists

Susan Arnold
171 Burnham Road
East Thetford, VT 05043
(802) 785-4248
www.folkfloors.com
folkfloors@valley.net

Linda Arthurs
Art on the Floor Studio
5 Mallory Gardens 803
Toronto, ON M4V 2A7 Canada
(416) 924-7295
www.artonthefloor.com
larthurs@home.com

Natalie Browne-Gutnik
8922 North Fielding Road
Bayside, WI 53217-1919
(414) 351-2389
www.floorcloth-natasha.com
natalie@floorcloth-natasha.com

Karen Calabrese
Karen's Art & Design
13580 87th Place North
Seminole, FL 33776
(727) 397-2729
www.KarensDesigns.com
KCDesign@tampabay.rr.com

Arlene Crooks-Best
Ar Works
88 Matilda Street
Stratford, ON N5A 6S1 Canada
(519) 271-5285
www.ar-works.com
beststrat@sympatico.ca

Linda Curran
Country Canvas
132 General Avenue
Ottawa, ON K1Z 7W8 Canada
(613) 729-2895
www.floorcloths.ca
floorcloths@home.com

Sandy Ducharme
Vermont Floorcloths
849 Ducharme Road
Marshfield, VT 05658
(802) 563-2745
hillcrestnursery@aol.com

Skip Dyrda
New World Productions
253 Links Avenue South
Sarasota, FL 34236
(941) 366-5520
www.emurals.com
painterskip@emurals.com

Lori Fusello
La Belle Epoque Studios
1812 Lombard Avenue
Everett, WA 98201
(425) 259-4889
www.labellestudios.com
labelle@labellestudios.com

Debra Gould
1260 Victoria Avenue
Victoria, BC V8S 4P2 Canada
(250) 418-8700
www.debragould.com
debra@debragould.com

Janet Harris
118 Bee Hill Road
Williamstown, MA 01267
harrysfavorite@juno.com

Mary Lou Keith
Studio 14
P.O. Box 1030
Shelburne, NS B0T 1W0 Canada
(902) 875-1333
www.studio14.ns.ca
studio14@klis.com

Linda Locke
Floorcloths of Arizona
527 West Lawrence Lane
Phoenix, AZ 85021
(877) 371-9300
www.floorclothsofarizona.com
lindalocke@qwest.net

Lisa Curry Mair
Canvasworks
326 Henry Gould Road
Perkinsville, VT 05151
(802) 263-5410
www.canvasworksfloorcloths.com
vtcanvas@vermontel.net

Pamela Marwede
629 Payne Parkway
Sarasota, FL 34237
www.Pamdesign.com

Orbo Design
PMB #281, 302 Bedford Avenue
Brooklyn, NY 11211
(718) 384-7404
www.orbodesign.com
rugs@orbodesign.com

Douglas Paisley
10 Main Street
Petersburgh, NY 12138
(518) 658-0434

Pam Richt Testerman
350 Berry Hollow Road
Gurley, AL 35748
www.floorclothsandmurals.com
PRTIRIS@aol.com

Alan Vaughn Studios
3961 North Ivy Road, NE
Atlanta, GA 30342
(770) 457-0820
alanvaughn@mindspring.com

Mail-Order Resources

Art Supplies and Canvas

Amsterdam Art
1013 University Avenue
Berkeley, CA 94710
(510) 649-4800

Daniel Smith
P.O. Box 84268
Seattle, WA 98124-5568
(800) 426-6740
www.danielsmith.com

Dick Blick
P.O. Box 1267
Galesburg, IL 61402-1267
(800) 447-8192
www.blickstudio.com

Flax Art & Design
1699 Market Street
San Francisco, CA 94103
(415) 552-2355
www.flaxart.com

Pearl Paint
308 Canal Street
New York, NY 10013
(800) 221-6845
www.pearlpaint.com

Utrecht
www.utrechtart.com
(800) 223-9132

Canvas and Floorcloth Patterns

Canvasworks
326 Henry Gould Road
Perkinsville, VT 05151
www.canvasworksfloorcloths.com

Latex Paint

Benjamin Moore & Co.
51 Chestnut Ridge Road
Montvale, NJ 07645
(800) 344-0400
www.benjaminmoore.com

Sherwin Williams
101 Prospect Ave. N.W.
Cleveland, OH 44115
www.sherwin.com

Stencils

Dreamweaver Stencils
1335 Cindee Lane
Colton, CA 92324
www.dreamweaverstencils.com
(909) 824-8343

Dressler Stencil Company, Inc.
253 SW 41st Street
Renton, WA 98055
(888) 656-4515
(425) 656-4381 FAX
www.dresslerstencils.com

The Stencil Library
Stocksfield Hall
Stocksfield, Northumberland
NE43 7TN
United Kingdom
+44 (0) 1661 844 844
www.stencil-library.com
info@stencil-library.com

Yowler & Shepps Stencils
3529 Main Street
Conestoga, PA 17516
(800) 292-5060
www.yowlersheppsstencils.com

Index

Other Storey Titles You Will Enjoy

Decorative Stamping, by Sasha Dorey. This book covers everything readers need to know to apply a wide range of decorative stamping techniques. Includes great ideas and easy-to-follow instructions for hundreds of unique and beautiful projects for the home. 96 pages. Hardcover. ISBN 0-88266-809-9.

Making Bent Willow Furniture, by Brenda and Brian Cameron. With this guide it's easy to make rustic bent willow furnishings for both indoors and out, such as a quilt ladder, plant stand, hanging basket, chair, porch swing, headboard, and more. 144 pages. Paperback. ISBN 1-58017-048-X.

Making Bits & Pieces Mosaics, by Marlene Hurley Marshall. Readers will learn how to use simple mosaic techniques to transform everyday objects into one-of-a-kind works of art by adding broken dishes, ceramics, and glass to various surfaces. 96 pages. Hardcover. ISBN 1-58017-015-3.

Nature Printing, by Laura Donnelly Bethmann. This book teaches readers the process of recreating images from the natural world by applying paint to leaves, flowers, herbs, or fruit and printing life-size forms onto fabric, paper, and other surfaces. 96 pages. Paperback with French flaps. ISBN 1-58017-376-4.

Paper Illuminated, by Helen Hiebert. As the popularity of handmade paper grows, this unique book takes the crafter beyond stationery, cards, and journals to innovative designs for using colored and textured paper to make three-dimensional home furnishings for a variety of settings. 144 pages. Paperback. ISBN 1-58017-330-6.

Rustic Accents for Your Home, by Laura Donnelly Bethmann and Ann Ramp Fox. With just a few simple tools and free or inexpensive materials, readers can bring nature indoors with these fun, creative projects. 128 pages. Hardcover. ISBN 1-58017-135-4.

Scarecrows, by Felder Rushing. Scarecrows are an American folk art that add charm and whimsy to any yard. This is the only book to offer instructions for creating them, from traditional to wild! 112 pages. Paperback. ISBN 1-58017-067-6.

Simple Fountains for Indoors and Outdoors, by Dorcas Adkins. Fountain designer and manufacturer Dorcas Adkins reveals her trade secrets for making 20 creative fountains — from a small, tabletop fountain to a full-sized waterfall — and at far less cost than buying them in stores and catalogs. 160 pages. Hardcover. ISBN 1-58017-190-7.

Stone Style, by Linda Lee Purvis. Readers will find dozens of wonderful, elegant projects and designs for the home using rocks, stones, and pebbles. From gift ideas to home accents, these creations will appeal to anyone interested in home decor, nature, or simplicity. 128 pages. Hardcover. ISBN 1-58017-375-6.

These books and other Storey Books are available at your bookstore, farm store, garden center, or directly from Storey Books, 210 MASS MoCA Way, North Adams, MA 01247 or by calling 1-800-441-5700. Or visit our Web site at www.storey.com